I0828324

Carl E. Braaten &
LaVonne Braaten

The Living Temple

A Practical Theology of the Body and the Foods of the Earth

WIPF & STOCK · Eugene, Oregon

Wipf and Stock Publishers
199 W 8th Ave, Suite 3
Eugene, OR 97401

The Living Temple
A Practical Theology of the Body and the Foods of the Earth
By Braaten, Carl E. and Braaten, LaVonne

ISBN 13: 978-1-5326-1267-1
Publication date 10/19/2016
Previously published by Harper & Row Publishers, 1976

To
Craig and Donna
Martha
Maria
Kristofer

Contents

Do you not know that your body is a
temple of the Holy Spirit within you,
which you have from God?
You are not your own;
you were bought with a price.
So glorify God in your body.

I Corinthians 6:19–20

And God said, "Behold, I have given you every plant
yielding seed which is upon the face of all the earth,
and with every tree with seed in its fruit;
and you shall have them for good."

Genesis 1:29–30

I will give no deadly medicine to anyone if asked;
. . . Into what ever houses I enter,
I will go into them for the benefit of the sick.

Hippocrates

The earth has enough for every man's need
but not for every man's greed.

Mahatma Gandhi

Preface

The Christian faith can be told from many perspectives. In this book we are building the message of the faith around the human body. We are reflecting the incarnational perspective of Christianity. In modern terms we could call it an essay on somatic theology —a religious somatology. The human body is linked to the good earth through the food that is eaten, the water that is drunk and the air that is breathed. Therefore, a theology of the body must also generate an ethical consciousness which takes concern for what agribusiness is doing to our food to get rich quick at the expense of our health, how big industry is destroying our earthly home to fatten itself at the risk of our human future, and how the healing professions are treating symptoms of illness with drugs and surgery, while often neglecting the care of the total person. And health care is so dispensed in our society that the poor and the not so poor can ill afford the expensive treatments.

We believe that Christianity today is called to announce and celebrate the sacredness of the body as the temple of the Spirit and to fight for its well-being on every front. The Spirit of God draws us more deeply into our bodies to care for them and to love others through them. The French have a saying, "To fit neatly into one's skin." We are concerned about our bodies because that's where we plan to spend the rest of our lives. The body is created by God very good and beautiful. When the Spirit comes, he does not lure us to seek life outside our bodies. The life of the Spirit flows incarnationally into the body of our Lord, becoming—as Luther called it—*Geistfleisch* (spiritual flesh). We are called to follow that incarnational current down to earth and into our bodies where we receive life and enjoy health.

Some years ago we became aware that the foods we were buying in the supermarket were not what they used to be. Some people around us had become very conscious about air and water pollution. But few seemed to realize that the greatest source of body pollution was from what we eat—the refined, processed, and chemicalized foods. For the sake of our family's health we began to look around for wholesome foods. Since there was no natural food store in our community, shopping meant driving miles away to locate the healthy foods we needed. That's when we came up with the idea of starting our own store, to bring natural foods into the community and make them available to our neighbors. Since then we have been involved in a process of learning more about the connections between the inner ecology of the body and the outer ecology of the earth.

Many of our friends in the natural and organic food movement bring a religious perspective to bear on their concern for body health. We have found among Jews, Muslims, Hindus, Buddhists, and people of other forms of Eastern mystical persuasion an elevated consciousness about what they put into their mouths. Among Christians those groups more closely oriented to the Old Testament, like Seventh Day Adventists, practice an awareness about health and nutrition in advance of their fellow Christians. As members of a church linked with the mainstream of the catholic tradition, we have felt an embarrassing lack of interest or knowledge on matters pertaining to the body. We have become convinced that there are unused sources in the Bible and the Christian tradition for the renewal and heightening of body consciousness. Particularly the doctrine of the Spirit in creation and incarnation can contribute to the making of a new body theology.

The whole person has a God-given natural right to whole food from the whole earth. Instead, every day brings us more bad news that the earth is being plundered and polluted, food is being processed and poisoned, and people are becoming more nervous and diseased. Living longer, they are enjoying it less. The quantity of life has grown by leaps and bounds, while the quality of life has been going downhill, for the rich as well as the poor. A theology of the body must be specially concerned about the earth and the food it yields, because the message of salvation on which Christianity rests comes to us in a sacrament of flesh (Jesus), in a sacrament of water (baptism), in a sacrament of food (bread), in a sacrament of drink (wine), and in a sacrament of persons (joint members of the body of Christ).

We are bringing together two perspectives which seldom make contact—theological conviction and nutritional wisdom. We are doing it not as a strained effort to join what our Western culture has separated, but as a natural outgrowth of our own day-to-day dialogue about faith and food, about religion and the body, about God and the earth, in short, about the relationship between the two fields to which our respective careers have committed us, namely, theology and nutrition.

Chicago, Illinois
August, 1975

CARL E. BRAATEN
LAVONNE BRAATEN

Introduction

On Bringing Theology Down to Earth

Books are filled with complaints that in the twentieth century Christianity has lost its soul. A different interpretation of the dramatic pace of change within the faith is possible. This is the century in which Christianity is discovering its worldly relevance. Think of such words as matter, earth, body, sex, world, history, and politics. They have entered into our common theological language as terms of approval, against the background of ages of alienation from the realities to which such terms refer. Christianity has been the victim of a creeping spiritualism which lures its devotees away from the joys of the present and their home in the body. But this is to forget that the biblical message does not call us to leave this world in favor of another. Rather, the story of the Bible is about the power of God entering this world and changing it from within the framework of the living body of humanity. The Christian mystery is not a revelation about the soul and its destiny in another realm. It tells about the future of God, his actions in the events of history and his embodiment in the everyday flesh and blood encounters of human beings.

There is a religious revival of sorts in the land which is homesick for old-fashioned supernaturalism and otherworldly religion. The Bible identifies such nostalgia as a sin against the promise of life to go forward in trust. The children of promise are not to long for the "flesh pots of Egypt." The distinctive thing about the Christian faith is that it speaks about the past and the future in terms of faithfulness to the present tasks and possibilities. It links the coming of God's kingdom to the flesh and blood existence of a human being. By divine election the body is the locus of the regenerating force of the Spirit. Christianity is the one truly incarnational faith among the religions of the world. Most of the other options tend to loosen the links of a person's identity with his body, pursuing the trail of the soul into the empty space of weightless existence. From the Christian standpoint we experience the presence of God in our bodies or not at all. For we are simply no-bodies without our bodies. As naked souls or spirits we do not and cannot exist.

When New Testament Christians talked about applying the benefits which Christ had won for all, they spoke of the Holy Spirit. What God has wrought in Christ for our sakes becomes really and immediately present through the Spirit. And the place where the fruits of the Spirit grow and mature is the body. As St. Paul says, the body is the temple of the Holy Spirit. Just as the Word became flesh in the first incarnation, so also the Spirit becomes humanly embodied in an ongoing incarnational process. We may call this the second incarnation—the incarnation of the Spirit of God for the redemption of our human body. The New Testament word for body in Greek is *soma*. We are more familiar with its use in psychology than in theology. But it is time now to stress the somatic dimension of faith and theology. For if we do not have theology of the body, other "ologies" will speak for the body, without caring for its ultimate religious meaning as the living temple of the Spirit.

Talk about the Spirit has become religiously fashionable. Everywhere people are asking about the charismatic movement. This is perhaps a sign of longing to enjoy some of the power of the Pentecostal experience. The apostles were turned on by the Spirit and became gifted in mission. Too often, however, the gifts of the Spirit are narrowed down to a few ecstatic experiences like speaking in tongues and healing by faith. There's enough of the Spirit to go around for everybody; no need for competition between different ways of being grasped by the Holy Spirit. Here we would plead for the works of the Spirit—equally miraculous—in the common life we enjoy in our bodies. Above all we would not restrict the working of the Spirit to what he may do in the hearts of an elect few. The Spirit is not working only at what Aquinas called "the sharp point of the soul," but wherever there is life. In the phrase of the Nicene Creed, the Holy Spirit is the One who gives life. He is the animating energy which makes the body live. Everything that concerns the living body becomes theologically relevant and ethically serious. This is what it means to bring theology down to earth—down to the level of the enfleshed Word and the somatic Spirit.

St. Irenaeus called the Word and the Spirit the "two hands of God" because they are the concrete ways by which God incorporates us into his life. God cannot be seen, but the operations of his Word in history and his Spirit in life can be heard and seen and felt in everyday things. He embodies for us the meaning of being human under the conditions of our earthly existence, not somewhere else. If we search the heavens for an encounter with God according to his absolute transcendence, we overshoot the mark and miss the place where God in his earthiness and human-mindedness chose to meet those who bear his image. In other words, we do not meet God at the top of a spiritual staircase but on the ground floor of somatic existence.

This is body-theology—seeking to follow the incarnational current that runs through the Bible from one end to the other. Here we have the movement of God in his self-incarnating transcendence, hence a descending transcendence, not the ascending transcendence so common in the great religions of the world. By way of mysticism they take off vertically into a spirituality that leaves the body behind, at best using it as a launching pad for an experience of spiritual ecstasy. For Christianity the criterion of the Spirit is not spiritual ecstasy but somatic wholeness. Holiness and wholeness go together. The saints are whole persons or their piety is but sanctimonious humbug. Health and salvation are not happening in different spheres, as though health is for the body but salvation for the soul. In Christian language we may just as well speak of salvation for the body and health for the soul, on the ground of the psychosomatic unity of the person and the wholeness of salvation. The solo religion of the soul in its individualistic odyssey into the empyrean of the gods and other immaterial entities is an old legacy of Gnosticism which many sick people in the West are currently trying to revive, only under new labels manufactured in the East.

There have been plenty of initiatives in modern culture to stimulate Christianity to rediscover its own original theology of the body. But theology has continued to wrap itself in an idealistic consensus going back to its Hellenistic period, which looks upon the body as the inferior part of the person. The spirit or the soul is the better portion, and it is to these immaterial, invisible, and intangible things that theology supposedly pays attention. No wonder that many theologians, floating on the clouds of these ethereal things, begin to feel the ground slipping out from under them. The subject matter of theology becomes elusive, perhaps illusory.

In theology we often look too hard for what is out of sight. Why not begin with the mystery posed by life itself in the human body? People are hankering for miracles of the Spirit, looking beyond the body for signs of his power and presence. In his book, *The Biology of the Spirit*, Edmund Sinnott reminds us of what the French philosopher, Henri Bergson, used to emphasize. Bergson urged us to see how the life of the body is on a continuum with the life of the spirit.[1] It was a fatal theological and philosophical error to isolate the spiritual life from all the rest, lifting it as high as possible above the earth. To avoid this Sinnott tries to reestablish the doctrine of the

Spirit on a biological basis. Theology becomes then a kind of metabiology.

Perhaps this biological approach can help theology to overcome that dualism of body and soul which made it captive to the idealistic consensus. When theology becomes unsure of its own ground and the reality to which it points, then it is well to remember that the body in which God is embodied is the same body which biology studies. The claim that they are different bodies is a heresy the Church Fathers called docetism. The docetists taught that the body of Christ only *appeared* to be a real human body; in essence it was nothing but a phantom.

From the premise that theology and biology deal with the same body, it follows that a number of other auxiliary studies can challenge theology to take its own body language seriously. Somatopsychic approaches to healing, bioenergetics, ecology, the organic revolution, the new science of nutrition and many other things invite theology to return home to the body and repent of having lusted after a spiritual union with God above and beyond his own incarnate habitation.

We may discover that in listening to the voice of the body as the medium of Spirit, theology will be on better terms with the Bible as well. For the Bible is truly a down-to-earth book, more materialistic than Karl Marx, except that it does not shave off the interesting edges of the body (ecstasies) that do not fit a purely horizontal scheme of things.

The New Testament proclaims the gospel of God's rule in the redeeming ministry of Jesus *in the flesh* and through his Spirit *in the body*. This is biblical language; no gospel apart from the flesh, apart from the body. The whole Christian faith, all of its great themes, can be organized around the concept of the body. John A. T. Robinson made a study of the theology of Paul in light of the *soma* principle. In *The Body, A Study in Pauline Theology,* Robinson says, "The concept of the body forms the keystone of Paul's theology."[2] Considering the human predicament, he speaks of this body of sin and death. As for the means of salvation, it is through the body of Christ on the cross. At baptism we are incorporated into his body the Church, and we are sustained by his body in the Eucharist. The new life in the Spirit is to be manifested in our body, and at last we are destined to be changed into the likeness of his glorious body through the resurrection. "Here, with the exception of the doctrine of God," Robinson says, "are represented all the main tenets of the Christian Faith—the doctrines of Man, Sin, the Incarnation and Atonement, the Church, the Sacraments, Sanctification, and Eschatology. To trace the subtle links and interaction between the different senses of this word *soma* is to grasp the thread that leads through the maze of Pauline thought."[3] For some reason this somatic dimension of Paul's theology has not been splendidly exhibited among those who prize his influence most highly.

We must still work for the liberation of the human *soma* from its schizoid condition in traditional-minded theology, where mind and spirit are pitted against body and nature. A person does not have a body; he is his bodily being from crotch to crown. A person is also spirit, but always *embodied* spirit. He is also a piece of nature, a lump of the earth, from dust unto dust, as Genesis 3:19 puts it.

The antisomatic prejudice of traditional Christianity continues to flourish in the preaching of the churches and the piety of their members. There is not much enlightenment of the body in theological schools, Christian congregations or at any of the levels of church leadership. Essentially the old Gnostic principle seems to govern our praxis: "Give to the flesh the things of the flesh and to the spirit the things of the spirit." Our modern semihuman Gnostics justify their contempt for the body by quoting Paul, "Flesh and blood cannot inherit the kingdom of God." (I Cor. 15:15). It is particularly distressing to see Christian leaders commit treason against their bodies. Dr. Paul Tournier writes, "All the churches speak of incarnation, but they generally suggest a contempt for the body, as if the spirit had debased itself instead of fulfilled itself in this wonderful venture that God has willed. We find in all our patients, especially in our pious patients, a certain contempt for the body."[4] Look at the ordained clergy of the churches! They pledge their lives to the gospel of Christ in the service of mankind. But they diminish their ministry to the extent that the bodies, in which they live and move and have their being, are half-dead—more like tombs than temples. Paul says, "Put yourselves at the disposal of God, as dead men raised to life; yield your bodies to him as implements for doing right" (Rom. 6:13 NEB). How ironic that those who bear the good news of the Spirit's redemption in the living human *soma* should drag themselves along in unfit bodies, out of shape and out of breath. It is not very edifying to hear about salvation from people who disdain the body's health. For salvation means health for man as a whole, body and soul.

Because theology had gotten itself lost in the clouds of the idealistic consensus, it was totally unprepared for the rise of somatic thinking in the nineteenth century. Consider its overreaction to the excesses of innovators like Darwin, Feuerbach, Marx, Nietzsche, and Freud[5]—all somantic thinkers who upgraded the body in the definition of being human. They all rebelled against the reigning theology in which the body counted for almost nothing. In the twentieth century theology has had to make the long trek home to the body where the faith was born in the first place.[6] One great help has been the rediscovery of Luther's down-to-earth theology. Luther loved the human orientation of God. Karl Barth caught the same message in his phrase "the humanity of God." The heart of God's concern is the good of man. For Luther a God without flesh was good for nothing, for as such he could only be the object of naked speculations. A God who is a being for thought alone does not have the same saving power as a God who can touch us in the flesh. So Luther preached the human form of God in Christ. As Christ himself said, "He who has seen me has seen the Father."

It is toward such a doctrine of God in man or of the Spirit in the body that we are aiming in this book. Only, in addition, we are urging a praxis of body-theology, a practical ethic of the body, to go with it. This has to do with total care of the body as the dwelling place of the Spirit.

NOTES

1. Edmund W. Sinnott, *The Biology of the Spirit* (New York: Viking Press, 1955), p. 130.

2. John A. T. Robinson, *The Body, A Study in Pauline Theology* (London: SCM Press, 1952), p. 9.

3. Ibid.

4. Paul Tournier, Preface to *The Meaning of the Body*, by Jacques Sarano, trans. James H. Farley (Philadelphia: The Westminster Press, 1966), p. 16.

5. For detailed discussions of these men as somatic scientists and philosophers, see Thomas Hanna, *Bodies in Revolt. A Primer in Somatic Thinking* (New York: Holt, Rinehart and Winston, 1970).

6. The somatic motif in contemporary theology has not yet reached its full potential, neither in dialectical nor in existentialist theology, and not yet in eschatological or process theology. But a good start has been made. Karl Barth went far to overcome the effects of Cartesian body/soul dualism in his doctrine of man. Oscar Cullmann followed suit in replacing the traditional Hellenistic-Christian idea of the immortality of the soul with the biblical doctrine of the resurrection of the body. And Rudolf Bultmann broke through to a new existential interpretation of *soma*, Paul's fundamental anthropological term. But for Bultmann *soma* meant nothing more than self—the self as personal subject relating itself to itself. *Soma* refers to this self-relating structure of individual existence. The result is amazing. The word *soma* has lost its meaning of concrete physical bodiliness. Paul Tillich was aware of the place of the body as a dimension of life, but basically he treated it as an organic condition for the emergence of the human spirit to which he then correlates the Spirit of God. Theology considers mainly what goes on at the contact points between the human spirit (with a small s) and the divine Spirit (with a capital S), chiefly religious, moral and cultural activities. But hardly anything like a theology of the body as such was elaborated in Tillich's systematic theology—which gives one to suspect that Tillich never became free of the idealistic consensus.

Among current theologians we find a new beginning in Pannenberg's recent essays on the doctrine of the Spirit. In building on Tillich's as well as Teilhard's views of life and the Spirit, not without offering a number of constructive criticisms to both, Pannenberg integrates the doctrine of the Spirit into the self-transcending quality of the body—a tendency that can be traced phenomenologically in all of life. He deplores the misuse of the doctrine of the Holy Spirit "as a fig-leaf to protect the nakedness of the Christian tradition from the questionings of modern critical thinking." (Wolfhart Pannenberg, *The Apostles' Creed in Light of Today's Questions* [The Westminster Press, 1972], p. 131.) For a renewal of the doctrine of the Holy Spirit Pannenberg says that a "theological penetration into the biological phenomenon of life would seem to be necessary" (ibid., p. 134). His aim is to show that really to understand the phenomenon of life, one eventually will have to get around to speaking of the Spirit of God.

I: The Temple of the Holy Spirit

Spirit as Energy

Talk about the Spirit becomes more prolific when people seek to spice up a dull life with a bit of mystery, miracle, or magic. They tend to look for clues to the Spirit in flashes of exotic experience, wherever the mind is breached by utterly weird and uncanny invasions. When religion itself becomes flat the Spirit is called upon to provide the fireworks. Joseph Sittler has called it "carbonated religion."

There is real fear in many churches of speaking about the Spirit. It could mean splitting the members into two classes, those who have the Spirit and those who don't. Some are merely baptized with water; others are baptized with the fire of the Spirit. The congregation is then divided between watered-down and fired-up Christians. The pastor is often caught between.

The Spirit faction is doing to the Church what the Church has done to the world—claiming the Spirit for itself and leaving the rest in the cold. Who has the Spirit? In traditional theology the Holy Spirit is the third member of the Trinity who usually remains idle until the Church gets born at Pentecost, or at least until that point in the history of salvation when Mary conceives and has a child. Pannenberg charges the Western tradition with limiting the Holy Spirit to the work of salvation.[1] The Spirit's role in the act of creation, as the energy of God breathing life into all his creatures, is neglected. This is true of Roman Catholic as well as Protestant theology.

According to Regin Prenter, an exception can be found in Luther's concept of the Holy Spirit. In *Spiritus Creator* Prenter shows that for Luther, on account of his biblical realism, the whole visible world is a creation of the Spirit. The Spirit is the power quickening all of life, the very same Spirit who mediates the real presence of Christ through Word and sacraments.[2] There's no restricting of the Spirit's creativity purely to the work of salvation. The force of the Spirit moves over the face of the waters, breathes into the nostrils of Adam the breath of life, and makes dead bones to rise again.

Since the work of Wheeler Robinson on Hebrew psychology[3] in the 1920s it has been widely recognized that the Greek distinction between body and soul has no support in biblical theology. In the crude mythopoetic language of the Old Testament there emerges a conception of the body-soul-spirit unity of man which stands opposed to orphic mythology and Platonic metaphysics. In the latter the soul is the prisoner of the body, of a totally different nature and destiny. For the Hebrews to say that man is a living soul or a living body comes to the same thing. Body and soul are not two disparate forms of existence which happen to get mixed up with each other for a brief spell on earth. Nor is salvation, as in the Hellenistic *soteria*, a matter of salvaging the soul from its dungeon in the body. The happiness of the soul is bound up with its somatic form of life.

The ancient Hebrew idea of the somatic essence of personality comes close to the idea of bodies as persons in modern philosophy. When Ludwig Wittgenstein says that "the human body is the best picture of the human soul"[4] or when Jean-Paul Sartre says that "I *am* my body to the extent that I *am*,"[5] they are echoing an idea at home on biblical soil. For the Hebrews a person's soul is in his flesh, in his eyes and ears, hands and feet, liver and heart, blood and breath, in short, in all his members and senses. In a famous dictum of Wheeler Robinson, "The Hebrew idea of personality is an animated body, and not an incarnated soul."[6]

Where does the Spirit of God fit into this conception? Nobody possesses the source of life in himself. As a sail cannot generate its own wind, neither can a person breathe life into himself. The Spirit is the wind of God, the Hebrews said. They called it *ru'ach*. The wind that blows is the breath of God. The special energy that drives a prophet, that's inspiration—the inbreathing of the divine Spirit. The Spirit is the principle of life in the human body, coming from an energy source beyond man, symbolically expressed by having to breathe in the air outside. To sum up, the body is the essential person, but his life comes from being in constant touch with the energies of God.

This Old Testament idea of the Spirit as the creative source of bodily life means that we can speak of the Spirit in the common life of people in the world. We do not have to adopt a spiritual tone and dwell upon psychic phenomena privy to a handful of pious people. The Spirit is at work in nature and in history, in creation and in redemption, in the individual and in the group, in culture and in religion, in the nation and in the Church. For the Spirit is the source of life—all life. The task of theology today is to liberate the Spirit from its confinement to the Church and to reclaim his life-giving power, not for souls alone, but for our bodies, their health and salvation.

Enfleshed in Man

The Spirit in the body of Adam and his family is intensely active in the flesh of Jesus and the new embodiment of his Spirit—the Church. In the end the Spirit will be poured out upon all flesh in an abundant way (Joel 2:8; Acts 2:17). At the present time, as most of us would confess, our share in the life of the Spirit is far from perfect. We are weak and sick, trapped in sin and death, yet boldly believing that the future of life and salvation for our bodies has already become present in the flesh of Jesus and the community nourished by His Spirit.

In stressing that the Holy Spirit is the universal principle of life in every human being, we would in no wise minimize the distinctiveness of his presence in the body of Christ. The claim to the universal validity of the Spirit of Christ is based on the fact that the life of every person in the world is a participation of the same Spirit. However, only in the flesh of Christ has there been a perfect unity with the Spirit. For all others, including the saints, the Spirit is fighting against the enemies of the body. There is such a thing as Satanic possession, where the body is ruled by forces opposed to the lordship of Jesus Christ. It is truly odd that people who know their Bibles should ever wonder whether there is such a thing as demon possession. Demonic possession is an extreme instance of a person becoming split in the depths of his being. In everybody there are signs of this condition. No one can claim to be fully free of the sickness that wreaks havoc with our bodies. Even a specimen of superhealth is stuck with a body that witnesses to this split condition in humankind.

Many people feel their bodies cause them so much trouble, they think of themselves as living in foreign bodies. This is the occasion, perhaps, for that dualism of body and soul so difficult to shake off. Can this body of mine really be me—the essential stuff which makes me who I am? Is it not only a wrapping which some day I hope to discard? Did not Paul himself cry out, "Who will deliver me from this body of death?" (Romans 7:24). Is not the body my chief obstacle, a bad companion, the source of so much suffering and torment? Does not life itself witness to the truth of that dualistic philosophy which equates evil with matter?

The feeling that my body is a stranger to me is not surprising, considering the universally human condition of estrangement. No one is perfectly reconciled with himself. There is an abyss, a lack, or a gap in each one of us. "All have sinned," Paul said, "and fall short of the glory of God" (Romans 3:23). Usually we suppose this refers to something going on in our spiritual lives. But not so with Paul. He emphatically stated, "You glorify God in your body" (I Cor. 6:20).

There's a war going on in our mortal bodies. But the body is not the source of evil or the cause of the estranged condition that erupts to separate us from ourselves, to make us feel split, soul against body in dualistic fashion. In the early Church there were Gnostics, and later Manichaeans, who taught that the soul is homesick because it has descended into a material body. It is struggling to get free of the flesh and this world of matter. Orthodox Christians answered, the body is good, not evil. We are not being diminished but fulfilled in the body. To be sure, sin is now permeating our bodies, making us feel like aliens in our own country. But sin is an invader from the outside; it has no right to make our bodies do its bidding.

We know that our bodies are essentially good, though they seem to torment us to death, because Christ has revealed God to us in the body. The incarnation of God is the revelation of the goodness of the body. We can affirm the reality of our own incarnation, because God has spoken to us in human language. The Word of God became enfleshed in man. This testimony is stronger than the id and all its feelings. When one's body feels filthy, like a bag of worms, as Luther once expressed it, remember, the true self is the body, the temple of the Spirit, the tabernacle of Christ. When we are tempted to disparage the body, make fun of it, or resent how it keeps us down to earth, let us consider the humility of God. For humility comes from the Latin *humus*, meaning of the earth, the soil.

The neo-Platonist philosopher, Plotinus, was ashamed to have a body; the Christian apostle, Paul, included the body in the essence of being human. Plotinus was a disciple of Plato who remarked, "the true philosopher is entirely concerned with the soul and not the body. He would like, as far as he can, to get away from the body ... to dissever the soul from the communion of the body."[7] In another place Plato has Socrates say, "And what is purification but the separation of the soul from the body, the release of the soul from the chains of the body ... ? True philosophers despise the body."[8] In this life, the wise man says, we ought to be busy loosening our ties with the body, because it's the soul that counts in the end.

This dualistic doctrine has been taught by Church fathers—and even by many Church mothers—as though it were the pure milk of the Christian gospel. So many Christians, striving for heaven, have longed for a state of disembodiment, thus reversing the earthward flow of the incarnation. They are tearing the soul or the spirit, or whatever it is they think worth saving, away from the totality of the real human being. Although traditional Christianity has affirmed the incarnation, it has fallen into a kind of double-talk, never willing to carry the carnalization of theology all the way down into the flesh. It has suffered from a gnostic hangover, splitting the human being into a higher and a lower part.

Where did this idea come from that the real person is not the body but the soul? It did not come from the Bible; it did not come from the Jews; it did not come from Jesus or Paul. It came from an old Greek myth and was believed 600 years before Christ. The myth tells about the making of man—where people came from. People came from the Titans. The Titans killed the son of Zeus, Dionysius, and they ate his flesh. Zeus got angry and killed the Titans; out of their remains sprang up the human race. Ever since there has been this Titanic element in man, this evil, earthy, physical being in the body, and there has been this other Dionysian element, this pure, spiritual, divine soul that longs to return home to the ethereal realm of the gods above. So the Dionysian ritual aims to help a person escape the prison of the body and rise to a union with god in a climax of mystical ecstasy. It has been possible to hid these ideas in the language of the Bible and pawn them off on the masses as the Christian hope.

The orthodox branch of Christianity, despite all its ambiguities, never completely swallowed the Greek myth about the soul. Somehow the good news of God pitching his tent in our bodies, and not merely our souls, has again and again broken through the hard crusts of asceticism, idealism, spiritualism, puritanism, and all kinds of isms that deny the enfleshment of God. In the words of Norman Brown, "The last thing to be realized is the incarnation. The last mystery to be unveiled is the union of humanity and divinity in the body.... Hence, to find the true meaning of history is to find the bodily meaning. Christ, the fulfillment, is not an abstract idea but a human body. All fulfillment is carnal."[9]

'Tis a pity that Ludwig Feuerbach covered up his true insight into the materialism of the incarnation with so much atheistic argument that Church theologians failed to hear the good he had to say. Feuerbach was fond of clipping out Luther-quotes and throwing them in the face of theologians. He believed the leverage of Luther would help him in his task of ridding theology of the remnants of idealism. He found in Luther's sermons a real sense of the bodily presence of God. The following quotation is typical of many: "Thus it is the noblest treasure and highest comfort we Christians have that the Word, the true, natural Son of God became Man, Who had flesh and blood just as any other man, and became Man for our sake, so that we might come to great glory, so that our flesh and blood, skin and hair, hands and feet, stomach and back may sit in heaven above, near God."[10] Feuerbach revolted against the abstract deity of speculative idealism, of making God a mere object of thought. So he said, "The God in your head is gas and wind; the God in Christ is a fixed and solid body."[11] Christ is the solid certainty of God's love for mankind; he has become bone of our bone and flesh of our flesh. "Say that you know of no other God," Luther said, "than the one Who lay in the womb of the Virgin Mary and suckled at her breast."[12] This was Luther's vivid way of assuring himself that God is no "bloodless phantom" who calls us to a fellowship of disembodied spirits. Even our warts look good to God, Luther said.

Body-Involving Liturgy

In the body we are individualized and personalized. Yet no one is wholly and only his body. He is always a member of a larger body together with others, as long as he is a living body. The alternative is to become a corpse, no longer capable of encountering others and enjoying bodily relationships. It is by means of the body that we are related to God and to the world around us. It takes on communal-relational meaning. In Paul's use of body language this is especially clear. By his body a person is an individual living in space and time. In his body he can perform the works of sin and evil, thus living according to the flesh. But also in his body he can live in a new set of relationships, act on new possibilities. "The body is . . . for the Lord (I Cor. 6:13), Paul said. Believers are united with Christ in a new body alive with the Spirit. This makes all the difference in how they live. Anything that competes with this new orientation of the body in unity with Christ is a sin unto death, like having sex with a prostitute, being circumcised after baptism, or eating meat in heathen temples, etc. For such things make the body a partner of deeds that do not spring from the new life in Christ.

The idea of being united with others in the body of Christ is symbolized for believers in the sacrament of eating bread. Christ took bread, broke it and gave it to his friends, saying, "This is my body." (Matt. 26:26). The body of Christ and sacramental bread become identified. The believer enters into union with Christ by means of the water in baptism and he celebrates that unity by sharing a meal of bread and wine with others. Eating and drinking —bodily events from top to bottom—become the most spiritual transactions in a person's life, and in the common life of a whole people. The people's liturgy is expressed in the ritual body,[13] in eucharistic bread and sacramental wine—mediating the presence of the great Name. The body is the *mysterium maximum*. Who dare condemn it?

The liturgical claim on the body has direct relevance to its involvements in real life. In Paul's day, as in every period of the church, including our own, there was a group of enthusiastic Christians who, in typical Gnostic fashion, held that they were so caught up in the Spirit, it was quite irrelevant what they did with their bodies. They operated with a kind of realized eschatology, fancying that they had already attained immortality, already in a position of transcendence above the mundane matters of the body. The body clings to the soul like a suit of old clothes ready for the grab bag. But it's so worn and tattered, it doesn't much matter what a person does with it anymore. So forget about the body's sexual purity; forget about holding a job; never mind what you eat. Against these Spirit-enthusiasts Paul said, the body is the real self. It plays a fundamental role in the new age which the Spirit has begun in the body of Christ. The body is redeemed and sanctified as an essential value in the future God has in store for us. Because the body is for the Lord, keep it holy until the parousia. The impending judgment will call each man to account according to the deeds performed in the body.

The enthusiasts at Corinth were scandalized by Paul's inclusion of the body in the sphere of Christ. Since the body for them lacked eschatological validity, there was no reason to care about its ethical meaning. But for Paul the body and spirit are one in the end. He coined the phrases "spiritual body" (*soma pneumatikos*). The body belongs to eschatological existence. In some way the eternal future of humanity will retain continuity with its bodily basis here and now. The body will be transformed, Paul says, spiritual, resurrected, glorified, but he has no way of telling us what these symbols mean in metaphysical terms. If the body is the necessary condition of communication and relationship here and now, it must also provide the symbolic data for the imagination in speaking of the eternal future of man. We may choose to remain silent, but in any case we have no way of speaking of naked spiritual existence without the body..

The impact of the term "spiritual body" is not metaphysical but ethical. Its payoff is not speculative but practical. As a symbol it affirms our faith in the goodness of the body. God created it good. It is the chosen seat of the Spirit of God and the very medium of our encounter with his Son Jesus Christ. This makes the body an excellent place to enjoy the gift of life. A negative attitude to the body leads to the breakdown of social order. Again Paul carried the argument to the pneumatic enthusiasts at Corinth. They did not discern the body, and so let a class distinction arise between the rich and the poor and between first- and second-class members in the congregation. The notion that God can be approached through mystical experience or esoteric knowledge by gaining distance from our bodies does violence to his real presence in the body to body relationships in the social order. "I was hungry, I was thirsty, I was a stranger, I was naked, I was sick, I was in prison."[14] These are all bodily relationships—food, water, shelter, clothes, medicine. We meet God in the body of such relationships with all our fellowmen. The seed of this concern for justice is respect for the body; the revelation of its dignity is the flesh of Christ; the stage of its enactment is the body of the world; the measure of its health is justice for all its weaker members.

Christians are called to walk the incarnational line in history. They are to be guided by the coming of Christ in the flesh and live according to the Spirit of his body. This does not mean getting all wrapped up in the second coming and guessing about the sequence of events surrounding doomsday. The Jesus-people and the Spirit-people of today are manifesting the same weariness with the world which betrayed the old Christian Gnostics into heresy. Instead of letting the Spirit drive us more deeply into our bodies, where we meet God in his perpetual humanity, spiritual enthusiasts would have us cut our ties with the body and the earth which feeds it.

They would have our souls take off into another kind of world, enjoying communion with God at the level of God in heaven, in contrast to the message of the Bible which shows God following the pull of gravity itself, coming down to earth, settling into our human skins, and holding fellowship with us at the level of flesh and blood.

The old Gnosticism is remaking its appearance in Western culture, by importing exotic varieties of the dualistic traditions of the East. Many Christians are susceptible to the highfalutin' talk about the soul in Eastern mysticism, because the Church has given them to believe that Christianity is essentially a message about the soul, only offering it the best chance of getting saved. A Western scholar once put the question to an old Caledonian islander whether it was not the idea of the soul which Christianity had brought to them. "No," was the unexpected reply, "we already know about that; what you have given to us is the notion of the body."[15]

Why are so many Christians dropping out of the churches and letting themselves get swept up by spiritual winds flowing in from the East? Some may say it is because the churches are not spiritual enough. In fact, the opposite is true; they are not somatic enough. Perhaps they occupy a no-man's land between body and spirit. We miss the body language of the gospel in the churches; others complain that they miss the excitements of the Spirit. So they are leaving the Church for the Eastern option. We are staying with the Church, demanding in the name of the gospel that it return home to the body.

NOTES

1. Wolfhart Pannenberg, "The Doctrine of the Spirit and the Task of a Theology of Nature," *Theology* 75 (1972), pp. 8–13.

2. Regin Prenter, *Spiritus Creator: Luther's Concept of the Holy Spirit* (Philadelphia: Muhlenberg Press, 1953), pp. 192–94.

3. H. Wheeler Robinson, "Hebrew Psychology," *The People and the Book*, ed. Arthur S. Peake (Oxford: Clarendon Press, 1925), pp. 353–82.

4. Ludwig Wittgenstein, *Philosophical Investigations* (New York: Macmillan Co., 1953), part 4, section 178.
5. Jean-Paul Sartre, "The Body," in *The Philosophy of the Body: Rejections of Cartesian Dualism*, ed. Stuart F. Spicker (Chicago: Quadrangle Books, 1970), p. 233. The selections in this chapter are taken from Sartre's *Being and Nothingness*.
6. Robinson, "Hebrew Psychology," p. 362.
7. Quoted by D. R. G. Owen, *Body and Soul* (Philadelphia: The Westminster Press, 1956), p. 39.
8. Ibid.
9. Norman Brown, *Love's Body* (New York: Vintage Books, 1966), pp. 221–22.
10. Ludwig Feuerbach, *The Essence of Faith According to Luther*, trans. Melvin Cherno (New York: Harper & Row, 1967), p. 71.
11. Ibid., p. 74.
12. Ibid., p. 87.
13. For a Jewish appreciation of the role of body in the liturgy, see Eric Gutkind, *The Body of God* (New York: Horizon Press, 1969).
14. Matt. 25:31–46. This is not a literal quotation.
15. The incident is related by C. A. van Peursen, *Body, Soul, Spirit: A Survey of the Body-Mind Problem* (London: Oxford University Press, 1966), p. 85.

A SELECT BIBLIOGRAPHY

Brown, Norman. *Love's Body*. New York: Random House, 1966.
Flew, Anthony, ed. *Body, Mind and Death*. New York: Macmillan Co., 1964.
Jonas, Hans. *The Phenomenon of Life, Toward a Philosophical Biology*. New York: Dell Publishing Co., 1966.
Owen, D. R. G. *Body and Soul*. Philadelphia: Westminster Press, 1956.
Pannenberg, Wolfhart. *What is Man?* Philadelphia: Fortress Press, 1970.
Robinson, H. Wheeler. *The Christian Doctrine of Man*. Edinburgh: T & T. Clark, 1911.
Robinson, John, A. T. *The Body*. London: SCM Press, 1952.
Sarano, Jacques. *The Meaning of the Body*. Philadelphia: Westminster Press, 1966.
Sinnott, Edmund W., *The Biology of the Spirit*. New York: Viking Press, 1955.

Tillich, Paul. *Systematic Theology*, vol. 3. Chicago: The University of Chicago Press, 1963.
Wingren, Gustaf. *Man and the Incarnation*. Philadelphia: Muhlenberg Press, 1959.
Walker, James Lynwood. *Body and Soul*. Nashville, Tenn.: Abingdon Press, 1971.

II: The Wisdom of the Body

A Holistic Approach

"Medicine has lost the sense of the person, the sense of man as a whole,"[1] writes Paul Tournier. He is a Swiss medical doctor and a lay theologian. His life's vocation was to promote medicine as a ministry of the whole person. In spite of advances in psychosomatic medicine and Gestalt psychotherapy, the sick person in our society is still most likely to fall into the hands of a medical specialist who takes a piecemeal approach to the body. The person is looked on as a physical object made of many parts. When the car breaks down, we take it to a garage and expect a mechanic to figure out which part needs to be fixed. Likewise, we treat our bodies like a machine. We go to a doctor and say, "I think it's my heart, doc," or perhaps the liver, a kidney or the prostate gland. The body has broken down and the trouble is localized in one organ. A drug is applied or surgery, or first one, then the other. It is imagined that sickness is something gone wrong with one of the parts of the body-machine. It makes sense then that medicine be practiced by superspecialists who know not the person as a whole but almost everything that can be known about one part of his anatomy. There is an old joke that the only difference between a doctor and a veterinarian is in the clientele.

A person cannot be whole and healthy by patching up the bits and pieces of a broken-down anatomy. For health lies not in the parts but in the whole. It's like salvation—one is saved as a whole in body, mind, and soul and not a piece at a time. Jesus of Nazareth was called the Great Physician because he made people "whole." Today a person who goes to the doctor hardly expects to be made *whole*. At best he hopes to get back on the road again but not as good as new. Or he may go to another healer who specializes in a different nook of the person's life—a psychologist, psychiatrist, psychoanalyst, or counselor of some kind. The result is the same—the person is parceled out and seen from a partial viewpoint.

Even the Gestalt movement in psychology, closely associated with the name of Frederick S. Perls, which prides itself on its holistic approach to human experience, fails to see the dimension of mystery, transcendence, of the "heart" in Pascal's sense of the word. In our view, the essence of the whole lies not in the person, in his own past or present, nor in the sum total of all his interpersonal relationships and involvements in the world. One may double or triple a purely materialist or naturalist view of the human being, but one will not reach thereby the essence of the whole, the aspect of eternity.

We can be grateful that humanistic psychology on its own has found it relevant to speak of the whole, of totality, of structural integration, of unity and the like. Such language is common to the theological tradition. But the whole is not given as a datum of human experience. Now we see only in part. Only from the standpoint of the final future of life can we be seen as a whole. Such a vision is a matter of faith and revelation. To be personally involved in the power of the whole is a gift of grace—the grace of the new life in Christ. The vision of the whole person and his absolute worth is tied to the wholeness of life and salvation in Jesus Christ. For he alone is the embodiment of the wholeness of God. This dimension of God's presence in the person of Jesus can contribute to the quest for a holistic perspective and help overcome the fragmenting of the person in the healing professions.

In the past theology has sought a dialogue with medicine, urging it to include more of the person than meets the eye. Gains have been made. No doctor would now deny the truth of psychosomatic medicine. The body influences the mind and the mind the body. A person can be caught in a vicious cycle where anxiety causes an ulcer and an ulcer may compound the anxiety. Glands and ideas often respond to the same stimulus. Anyone scared or in love knows that. A pure mechanistic materialism has long since been superseded, at least in theory though often not in practice.

Still, there is something more, theology would insist. That is the dynamics of the Spirit in personal life. If we think of a cone-shaped pyramid, the physical life forming the base and the spiritual life the peak, theology has usually wished to draw physiological and psychological sciences to engage in dialogue at the level of peak experiences. This has been a fatal mistake on the side of theology. It has led theology to restrict its concerns to the vanishing point, or at least to such a fine point of the soul that many people either deny it exists or claim to have enjoyed no such summit meetings with the Spirit. The background of this fatal mistake is the dualism of body and soul. As long as people believed in the soul, theology was in business. The moment the existence of the soul was denied, skeptics and believers alike imagined that theology had lost its theme.

The Spirit of God does not come in at the top, at the point of peak experiences. Nor is the body far down at the base, farther from the Spirit than the mind or the soul. Throughout we have countered the view that the body is less spiritual than the soul. The Spirit is not confined to the upper story of human experience—the religious or mystical realm. The Spirit of God does not make contact with a faculty in man called the spirit or the soul. The Spirit is the power of wholeness, giving meaning, unity, direction, and destiny to the somatic self in this sinful, broken, and diseased world.

The body itself is spiritual fact. The essence of a person lies not in himself but in being open to the Spirit who shares with us the embodied wholeness of God in Jesus the Christ—our Savior and Healer.

Theology must move down the scale and engage in dialogue with those who try to heal at the base of somatic existence. We should not ask doctors to become more spiritual, rather for theologians to become more somatic in their perspective, thus overcoming the heresy of angelism in their own heritage. Angels don't have bodies. A holistic approach to health calls for theology to take more seriously the life of the Spirit in the body. Bad habits, bad food, bad air, bad water, overeating, overdrinking, oversleeping, overworking —all these are threats to the incarnation of the Spirit in human life. We have seen theology squeeze hard such words as spirit, will, mind, soul, ego, guilt, fear, dread, anxiety, loneliness, alienation, frustration for all their worth and meaning. However, the whole person is more than a bundle of psychic functions. He is also a living bodily being—laughing, loving, sweating, secreting, oozing, scratching, grunting, touching, tasting, bleeding, itching, aching, pulsing, throbbing, breathing, panting, growing, dying. This is the original language of the body, and no matter what a person says with words, the body does not lie.

When a person becomes sick, he is speaking the language of the body. He may conspire with the doctor to objectify and localize the illness in one organ. But deep down he knows that when one member suffers the whole is sick. The painful organ is but giving voice to the whole suffering body. He feels relieved when the doctor can put his finger on the right spot, diagnose what's wrong and write out a prescription. That way there is no risk, no encounter, no dialogue between patient and physician. Both have failed to decode the message and the day of reckoning has been postponed. Having driven out one demon, seven others rush in and, as Luke the physician reports, "the last state of that man becomes worse than the first." (Luke 11:26). Every sick person is crying out for a double diagnosis, first, a medical diagnosis of the organ in trouble, and second, an interpretation of the person as a whole, how he lives and what he eats, how he sleeps and recreates, how he works and exercises, how he prays and what he dreams of, his sex and family life, his hates and loves and fears and hopes—all these things are elements in a therapy of the whole person.

Physician, Heal Thyself!

In classical times the task of the doctor was to teach people how to live in accordance with nature. There are certain laws of life etched into the natural wisdom of the body. Pythagoras, the forerunner of Hippocrates, the Father of medicine, taught that health is harmony of life and disease is the loss of equilibrium. He also taught that food can contribute to peace of mind as well as the health of the body. Hippocrates, too, defined medicine as the art of getting people to reform their lives. If a person becomes sick, it means that he is doing something wrong. What good does it do to heal a person with a shot in the arm, if he goes on repeating the folly that made him ill in the first place? We ask our doctors to give us drugs. That's what they are trained to do. After all, they studied *medicine.* The average patient would perhaps be shocked if his doctor took the time to teach him the wisdom of the body and the laws of healthful living which our modern lifestyle is constantly ignoring.

When we speak of laws of healthful living, this does not mean that a person can be promised health by following a set of fixed rules about eating, exercising, working, and resting. Health involves the synergizing of many factors and functions—bodily, psychic, and spiritual. Paul said that if a person does all the right things, but has not love, it's all good for nothing. A person may try so hard to do the thought that they may do something wrong. Here the person has become the servant of the law, and the joy of life has been expelled. Although this book is more concerned with the human soma and its earthly connections, we would not forget the divine power of healing through faith and the reconciling power of love to make a person whole. Sin is the root cause of all human sickness, and only the gospel has the power to penetrate its depths.

The tragedy of the modern approach to health and disease is the fact that medicine has separated itself from religion. In breaking away from the priesthood, it has established itself as a pseudo-priesthood in modern society. People have more faith in what doctors do and what doctors recommend than they have in the gospel, even those who go to church and profess otherwise with their lips. TV ads capitalize on this wildest of American superstitions. Admen wouldn't spend millions of dollars on nonsensical commercials if they couldn't count on true believers out there to buy their pharmaceutical poisons.

Christianity was born as a religion of healing. Jesus said, "Heal the sick, raise the dead, cleanse lepers, and cast out demons" (Matt. 30:18). One of the four evangelists, Luke, was a physician. In Christian history many of the saints—over sixty—were also doctors. This connection has been maintained to the present time by the medical missionaries—the Albert Schweitzers and many other unsung heroes of the faith. To our surprise we came upon a book by John Wesley, the great eighteenth-century evangelist-reformer and founder of Methodism, entitled *Primitive Remedies*. We never learned in church history that John Wesley was a kind of Dr. Spock of 200 years ago, writing a standard home doctor book for the common people. What he says in this old book still makes a lot of sense. It's almost as though Wesley were writing in New York, Los Angeles, or Southside Chicago when he says, "The air itself that surrounds us on every side is replete with shafts of death; yea, the food we eat daily saps the foundation of that life which cannot be sustained without it."[2] He states that because of man's rebellion the scene has changed for the bad, but by the art of medicine we can soften the evils of life and prevent the sickness and pain to which we are exposed. To this end he recommends, in addition to proper exercise, work, and temperance, "that kind and measure of food which experience shows to be most friendly to health and strength."[3]

Wesley wrote his book as a protest against the medical trends of his time. He charged that medicine had become an abstruse science beyond the reach of ordinary men, and doctors were being admired as "something more than human."[4] Besides their great prestige they now worked for profit, exacting huge fees from the people. This is all contrary to the "Oath of Hippocrates" wherein the physician says that "I will give no deadly medicine to anyone if asked" and "into whatever houses I enter (doctors seldom enter houses anymore), I will go into them for the benefit of the sick" and "without fee or stipulation." Neither Wesley nor anyone else would deny the doctor the right to a good living, but because of their new-found honor and wealth they "were keeping the bulk of mankind at a distance."[5]

Let us attend to Wesley's complaint a bit further. The doctors have

> "filled their writings with abundance of technical terms, utterly unintelligible to plain men. . . . They introduced into practice abundance of compound medicine consisting of so many ingredients, that it was scarce possible for common people to know which it was that wrought the cure; abundance of exotics; neither the nature nor names of which their own countrymen understood; of chemicals, such as they neither had skill, nor fortune, nor time to prepare; yea, and of dangerous ones, such as they could not use without hazarding life, but by the advice of a physician. And thus both their honor and gain were secured, a vast majority of mankind being utterly cut off from helping either themselves or their neighbors, or once daring to attempt it."[6]

fetched medicines that were too dangerous for a wise person to fool with, but served "only to swell the apothecary's bill."[7]

Switching to the present we can say that the most oppressed class in American society are the sick. Those who believe in the gospel of healing should, like John Wesley, lead a patients' revolution against the establishment of organized medicine in the United States. There's hardly a family who cannot tell a few horror stories based on personal experience in making the rounds of doctors in quest of healing. Recent studies show a growing disenchantment of ordinary people with the medical practices of our time. It seems like the real biblical literalists are the doctors of today, for when it says, "If thy hand offend thee, cut it off... if thy foot offend thee, cut it off... and if thine eye offend thee, pluck it out" (Mark 9:43, 45, 47), we are witnessing a literal execution of such imperatives in the modern butchery called surgery. The easiest thing to do is to cut off an organ. It is much more difficult to grow a new one. Why are surgeons so quick with the knife? Is it because it pays better or that they know no better? The natural methods of nutritional corrective are slower but the results are often more satisfying in the long run.

Many doctors are woefully deficient in knowledge about nutrition and what it can do for themselves and their patients. That is not a blanket indictment of the medical profession. A great deal has to be said about the areas in which real progress has been made. Antibiotics are effective against certain diseases and many of the conspicuous scourges have been virtually conquered like diptheria, smallpox, and poliomyelitis. Nor would we deny that there is a place for drugs and even surgery in emergency situations. But today emergency situations have become all too routine. Overdrugging is common and the knife-happy surgeon is an easy prey to greed. One statistic: over 20 percent of the patients in hospitals are there from effects caused by drugs prescribed by doctors.[8] Oftentimes the cure proves more lethal than the disease.

Medical orthodoxy so far has virtually ignored the nutritional approach to healing. Most medical schools do not teach courses in clinical nutrition. They learn the standard bit about scurvy, beriberi and pellagra being caused by nutritional deficiencies. But their orientation is more to drugs than foods when dealing with noninfective diseases. Somewhere along the line medicine took the wrong turn in the road, looking not to nature but to the laboratory to provide a cure for every ailment.

The drugs we take usually cover up the condition for which we seek the doctor's help. Americans spend $120 million on laxatives each year. Last year they ate over 5000 tons of aspirin, but let's face it, an aspirin can only make you forget your headache. It masks the symptoms, but leaves the cause alone. A headache is trying to tell a person that something is wrong and he had better deal with it. Covering it up, like in the case of Watergate, only postpones the day of judgment. Likewise with the tons of sleeping pills, pep pills, tranquilizers, reducing pills, laxatives, and antacids —they may bring temporary relief but fail to get at the real difficulties. In covering up the symptoms they are gagging the body which is speaking the only language it knows.

By Their Fruits Ye Shall Know Them

Americans are as healthy as their diet. Their diet is bad and getting worse and America is rapidly becoming a nation of sick people. But don't we have more hospitals and doctors for our population than other nations? Yes, but Plato said in his *Republic* that the need for many hospitals and doctors is the mark of a bad city. The United States ranks no better than eighteenth in terms of infant mortality and twenty-first in life expectancy. More important, however, than the quantity of our years is the quality of our life. Medical technology is able to extend the life of a sick person by a few years. But what we want, in the words of Dr. Paul Dudley White, is tality people traditionally long for. While the standard of living has been increasing, the quality of life has been going down. Gradual decay has been taking place, not only in our cities but in our bodies. The growth of technology has given us false trust that things are getting better and better. To be sure, technology has given us new techniques in sanitation, antiseptics and surgery. But the degenerative diseases have been quietly galloping to epidemic proportions.

We do not wish to bore the reader with statistics. They can be notoriously manipulated to fit any thesis. But for what they're worth, consider that over half a million Americans died of heart attacks last year. Think of all the people dragging along with heart conditions, estimated to be over 27 million. That means one out of every eight persons has a disease of the heart or blood vessels. Over seven million have some kind of arthritis or rheumatism. One out of every ten American men has a stomach ulcer. Millions are suffering from diabetes and hypoglycemia. Add to these all the other chronic disorders, asthma, anemia, obesity, multiple sclerosis, cancer, senility, nervous and mental diseases, alcoholism, and respiratory difficulties, and you get a picture of a nation being crippled by disease to a degree that is almost unbelievable.

Many a person thinks he is healthy because he never spends any time in the hospital or the doctor's office. But what is one's conception of health? The mere absence of a crippling or killing disease? People have come to think that it is natural to be sick or sickly, to have at least one thorn in the flesh. It may be just hemorrhoids, varicose veins, high blood pressure, hernia, overweight, insomnia or constipation; the condition has become so chronic the person has forgotten the feeling of positive well-being, radiant health, and a buoyant spirit.

The Devil Theory

The common view which people have is that germs cause disease. Ever since the Garden of Eden men and women have blamed their afflictions on the enemy outside. Adam said, "Eve made me do it" and Eve said, "The devil made me do it." We say, "I caught the flu bug," or "Somebody gave me a cold." We are bent on blaming the world outside for the miseries we experience. Either we inherited a weakness or the environment is hostile, but if we are sick it's not our fault.

Louis Pasteur acquired immortal fame in medical history by discovering that germs cause disease. He found microbes, tiny organisms, that cause food to spoil and produce disease. The germ theory, at first rejected as heresy by the medical authorities of that day, now enjoys the status of orthodox doctrine. As surely as there is truth in this theory, it has been greatly overworked. We look for germs or viruses to explain all our ills like the old voodooists with their evil spirits. Our enemies—these evil germs—are prowling around seeking someone to devour (I Pet. 5:8). The task of medicine is to find the germs, to kill or drive them out and thus save the victim.

There is no doubt that diseases are caused by germs and that sometimes drugs do work against these foreign invaders. We are continually being bombarded by bacteria in the environment. We never know when we'll be attacked by surprise and struck down by one of the plagues, if not the angel of death itself, against which we had insufficient resistance to fight successfully. But germs don't explain everything. As husband and wife we have experienced that one gets sick and the other doesn't. But we breathe the same air, sleep in the same bed, and eat the same food. Why do the germs love the body of one more than the other? We can't explain that, unless there is something going on in the body to lower its resistance or to increase its susceptibility to the attacking germs. There is the internal environment of the body that can spell the difference between health and disease. If the body is under stress, weakened by toxins or malnourished, it tends to become overly hospitable to it all. When the Dutch scientist went to Java to study beriberi, he searched in vain for the microbe that caused the disease. As it turned out, it was not the *presence* of an enemy but the *absence* of a friend—vitamin B—that brought on the paralysis. Today, the search for the cause and the cure of cancer is at a dead end. Could it be that it has nothing to do with a virus that many well-paid scientists have been looking for? Or could it be a nutritional deficiency—vitamin B_{17}—that another group is proposing? Vitamin B_{17} is called Laetrile, an extract of apricot pits, the use of which the medical establishment opposes and which the government has declared illegal. Pro-Laetrile groups have argued "that cancer is a multi-billion-dollar industry that would be ruined if it could be shown that cancer is (like scurvy, rickets, pellagra, pernicious anemia, beriberi, and other maladies) a vitamin-deficiency disease, and that medical orthodoxy and bureaucratic officialdom were protecting this industry."[10] Otherwise how can it be explained that the politics of medicine frantically opposes even scientific testing of Laetrile on human beings? What do the cancer politicians have to defend, except a very poor record in face of the staggering fact that a million Americans are now under medical care for this disease? One ought to think twice next time he is asked to make a donation to cancer research.

Nutrition experts as well as friends of the natural-food movement, like Senator Proxmire, frequently complain about the opposition of the medical establishment to research into the nutritional origin of disease. It can point to an admirable record of progress in combating infectious diseases, but its performance in preventing and curing the degenerative diseases deserves an F. Yet, the bulk of the doctor's patients falls into the latter category. It is tragic that the patient's maximum need should coincide with the physician's minimum competence. The cost is high in terms of human suffering and medical bills.

The Ecology of Health

The road to disease is paved by the food we eat and the drugs we take. If someone were to imagine a lifestyle guaranteed to insure a diseased body, he would be well-advised to build his model on our national example. For a start he would take the attitude reported of one young doctor who believed "that the body could get all the nutrients it needs from hot dogs, french fries, and Cokes, so long as the person is kept free from hunger."[11] Like driving into a gas station, we stand up to the counter and say, "Fill 'er up!" But we are more careful about our cars than our bodies. If the attendant were to put sand or water in our tank, we'd become angry. If we get handed a bunch of chemicals, we take and eat. No one would expect a horse to win the Kentucky Derby on a diet equivalent to french fries, hot dogs, and ice cream. How then can we hope to run a good race and fight a good fight on the kind of garbage we put into our stomachs?

The first thing we would underscore in the ecology of health is a good nutritious diet, with the right balance of proteins, fats, and carbohydrates, high on vitamins and minerals, especially in the form of raw fruits and vegetables. It bears mentioning again that whole foods, natural and organically grown foods are far superior to the partial foods, the refined, processed, and chemically adulterated products. Above all, a person is eating himself right into the grave if a large part of his diet comes from the empty calorie foods made of white sugar and white flour. Cut them out and learn to eat seeds, nuts, and whole grains. The power of life is found in the germs of plants. If a person's diet has been reformed he will learn how to use the wonder foods—yogurt, Brewer's yeast, wheat germ, and lecithin—and find himself liberated from the wonder drugs. Food is a better buy than medicine.

But we cannot live by bread alone. We must also drink water, but pure and uncontaminated water is hard to find. Water has two functions, to cleanse the body and provide it with minerals. The vater supply in most of our large cities is polluted, either from ieavy metal poisoning, insecticides, or fluorides. Chlorine kills ;erms but also the enzymes. Many have taken to drinking distilled vater, but that is void of the minerals we need. Water softeners emove the hard minerals and result in drinking too much sodium, vhich studies have linked up with so much heart trouble. The best olution is to buy pure natural spring water with all its minerals.

As important as what we eat and drink is the way we do so. Many of us are doing most things wrong. We eat when we are not eally hungry and drink when we are not thirsty. We eat many big neals and gulp them down in a tense atmosphere. We flush the food lown with liquid when it should be chewed slowly and partially ligested before it reaches the stomach. We should never eat when ve are tired or taxing our minds with weighty decisions. The busiiess and committee meetings we hold over lunch place burdens ipon our stomachs and hasten the day when we either will have to lrop out or drop dead.

It would be better for a busy person to take a break at noon for xercise and relaxation than to load up the system with calories and ocktails. Our sedentary lifestyle is softening our bodies and making them easy pushovers for the diseases of civilization. Studies on ats have shown that when they are kept in a small warm cage they ecome fat and flabby. Rats that live in larger cages get plenty of xercise and remain nice and trim. The motto of our age is never un when you can walk, never walk when you can ride, never stand vhen you can sit, never sit when you can lie down. Our primitive orebears had to do physical work for food and take care of the other necessities of life. They were not obese. The thermostat that ontrols our weight does not function properly without physical xercise. It seems that the whole system gets clogged up; the muscles lose their tone, the organs get sluggish, the glands become lazy, nd blood circulation slows down. By proper exercise we have beter control of our breathing and our cells and tissues receive the oxygen they need to keep us well.

Speaking of oxygen, there's a point to the joke about the city boy who took a trip into the country and remarked, "Fresh air smells funny." The human being has by nature—by God!—the right to clean fresh air. If the laws of a society cannot guarantee a person his natural rights, they have ceased to deserve our respect. Air pollutants—solid particles and noxious gases—are getting into our lungs and taking our breath away; our cars are to blame and also the big industries. The big corporations are spending more money buying TV commercials telling us how much they love our environment than they are on mending their filthy ways. As the energy crisis gets worse, it will force the industry to bring cars down to the size we need and quit our wanton wasting of fuel.

There is not much each of us can do immediately about pollution in the external environment. Personally, we could move to the country, but our jobs are in the city. One thing we can do, meanwhile, and that is to keep the inner environment of the body as clean as possible. Can anyone doubt any longer that smoking causes cancer and heart attacks? As long as moralists told us that it was wrong to smoke, we had to puff on a cigarette to prove our Christian liberty. But when scientists proved that smoking was quite a reliable method of committing suicide, we struggled to quit. It paid off. Food began to taste better, the lungs could breathe more easily, smoker's cough went away, we got fewer colds, nerves calmed down and we could get to sleep better at night. We also learned—the hard way—that the smoking advertisements are all lies. Smoking doesn't make a person look real cool and sexier; it doesn't give him a lift or steady his nerves; and it doesn't keep the weight down. In fact, it doesn't do a thing except damage one's health. Besides, if a person takes a total approach to body health, it is not that difficult to quit. One nutritionist recommends a three-day fast as the beginning of a good cure, and a lot of other toxins will be discharged in the process.

What Must We Do To Be Saved?

We have tried to paint a picture of optimum health in a sick world. We believe that we must accept responsibility for our own lives, and that we can't wait for government, organized medicine, the schools, or the big food companies to tell us how to live, what to eat or how to prevent disease. We are actually living in the dark ages when it comes to body culture. Culture is too fine a word for the conditions under which we live. We rear our youth in almost total ignorance about the fundamental arts of life: gardening, cooking, eating, working, playing, exercising, meditating, praying, and making love. The schools teach all the facts of life, but what do we as teachers know about the arts of life? What our children have been taught about health and nutrition in school, for example, has to be almost entirely unlearned again at home. Propaganda for the large corporate interests has been smuggled into the curricula as education.

A reunion of the person with his body and of the body with the natural foods of the earth is a condition for the actualization of the Christian vision of the whole person. These facets of living according to nature have been neglected both in our theory of the good life and our behavior patterns. Our disregard of the axioms of health in respect to the inner ecology of the body and its earthly environment has led to a situation in which man has misplaced himself in the world. The result is an uneasiness; man is dis-eased in the body and ill-at-ease in the head. He is out of harmony with himself, his fellowman, his Creator and the world of nature with which he lives.

The question arises: what must we do to be saved? Culturally speaking, we are on the road to damnation. Our healing professions are betraying us. We have entered the age of dietary anarchy. Parents are feeding their children food unfit for human consumption, actually much worse than we feed our pets. Many a woman beating the drums for "women's lib" has given up home cooking for factory-prepared foods, thinking that she is buying freedom. That crack needs to be balanced by saying that a man's place is in the kitchen, as much as the woman's. A man ought to make sure his food is not poisoning him to death. Richard Talbot tells of his trip to St. Petersburg, Florida. The place is full of lonely widows. They have outlived their husbands. Why? He pondered and then said to himself: "I'm willing to wager that everyone of these widowed ladies is a superb cook. What sumptuous, delicious, mouth-watering dishes and desserts they must have prepared and concocted for their deceased husbands while they were married. Oh, how well they practiced the art of cooking. So well, in fact, that every one of them cooked her husband's goose."[12]

Christians ought to reclaim their message of healing for the whole person and the salvation of the body. Christianity has an inner commitment to fight against the modern demons that lead to decay, degeneration, and death. It is a message of life, of hope for a new age, of promise for an era of maximum health and spiritual development. Christianity ought to stress anew that it is a religion of hope for the whole man and the whole earth. This includes the healing of the biosphere, because man's health depends on a sane ecology. Mankind cannot be whole and healthy in a world that is foul and filthy. Each person can join the revolution for a new way forward by minding what he puts into his own body. Becoming healthy means becoming sane and sound, unifying one's bodily, mental, and spiritual functions. In Jesus Christ we have the announcer and bringer of a new reality that makes us hope and work for the conversion and transformation of all that is old. The promise of new reality will not let us surrender to despair in the midst of this dying world. For in Christ the kingdom of God has appeared, and its nature is salvation, healing of all that is ill, making whole what is degenerate.

NOTES

1. Paul Tournier, *The Whole Person in a Broken World* (New York: Harper & Row, 1964), p. 38.
2. John Wesley, *Primitive Remedies* (Beverly Hills, Calif.: Woodbridge Press Publishing Company, 1973), p. 10.
3. Ibid.
4. Ibid., p. 13.
5. Ibid.
6. Ibid., pp. 13–14.
7. Ibid., p. 16.
8. Alan H. Nittler, *A New Breed of Doctor* (New York: Pyramid House, 1972), p. xiii.
9. E. Cheraskin and W. M. Ringsdorf, *New Hope for Incurable Disease* (New York: Exposition Press, 1971), p. 139.
10. Michael L. Culbert, *Vitamin B-17—Forbidden Weapon Against Cancer* (New Rochelle, N.Y.: Arlington House, 1974), p. 24.
11. Alan H. Nittler, *A New Breed of Doctor*, p. 114.
12. Richard Talbot, *How To Succeed With Your Own Body* (Oceanside, Calif.: Mr. Health, Inc., 1973), p. 4.

A SELECT BIBLIOGRAPHY

Abrahamson, E. M., and Pezet, A. W. *Body, Mind and Sugar.* New York: Pyramid Books, 1951.

Adams, Ruth, and Murray, Frank. *Megavitamin and Therapy.* New York: Larchmont Books, 1973.

Airola, Paavo. *How To Get Well.* Phoenix, Ariz.: Health Plus Publishers, 1974.

Alsleben, H. Rudolph, and Shute, Wilfrid E. *How to Survive the New Health Catastrophe.* Anaheim, Calif.: Survival Publications, Inc., 1973.

Bircher, Ruth. *Eating Your Way to Health.* London: Faber and Faber, 1961.

Cheraskin, E.; Ringsdorf, W. M.; and Clark, J. W. *Diet and Disease.* Emmaus, Penn.: Rodale Books, 1968.

Krugler, Hans J. *Slowing Down the Aging Process.* New York: Pyramid Books, 1973.

Marsh, Edward E. *How to Be Healthy With Natural Foods.* New York: Arco Publishing Co., 1967.

Nittler, Alan H. *A New Breed of Doctor.* New York: Pyramid House, 1972.

Null, Gary et al. *Body Pollution.* New York: Arco Publishing Co., 1973.

Pauling, Linus. *Vitamin C and the Common Cold.* San Francisco: W. H. Freeman and Co., 1970.
Tournier, Paul. *The Healing of Person.* New York: Harper & Row, 1965.
Wade, Carlson. *Nature's Cures.* New York: Award Books, 1972.
Williams, Roger. *Nutrition Against Disease.* New York: Pitman Publishing Corporation, 1971.

III: Foods for Life

Christianity and Food

Christianity has never made a dogma out of diet. From the beginning it liberated believers from the food laws which Moses had formulated for the children of Israel. Christianity is the only one of the great world religions which keeps faith and food separate. Judaism and Mohammedanism, as well as the Eastern religions, Hinduism and Buddhism, all integrate rules for feasting and fasting into their beliefs and practices. To be sure, Christianity has not remained totally silent. Until recently, Roman Catholics were not to eat meat on Fridays, and during Lent many Christians still encourage some form of fasting. In the New Testament the apostle Paul forbade Christians to eat meat offered to heathen idols, because that would put them in league with demons. But he had nothing against eating meat as such. As for drinking wine, he taught that a moderate amount is good for the stomach.

On the whole, however, the references to food and drink in the New Testament are few and of no importance for faith and morals. The historic position of Christianity was already stated in the Gospel of Mark. Jesus is quoted as saying, "Do you not see that whatever goes into a man from outside cannot defile him, since it enters not his heart but his stomach, and so passes on?" (Mark 7:18–19). To this Mark adds his editorial comment, "Thus he declared all foods clean."

Believing that all foods are clean, Christians have eaten whatever they please. They have boasted of their freedom from the dietary laws of the Old Testament. In fact, the newness of the New Testament consists in no small measure of being free from the religious taboos on food. The gospel cuts away the hedge which religion has built around certain foods, and declares them all good. The gospel is the power to demythologize food, clearing away the rules and rituals which make it man's master; it once again places him in charge of the garden. The gospel reaffirms that the food of the earth is good. Food is made for man and not man for food.

If that were all, we could rejoice in the gospel and go on eating as we please. We could continue to trust that food is clean, that it's not what goes into the stomach that defiles a man. But we know better now. Man is no longer eating food under garden conditions. Our food can no longer be declared clean. If a person doesn't watch out, he can easily defile himself with what he puts into his mouth. Jesus was not a modern man. He had no need to warn against eating garbage and drinking poison. He did not know that one day the rich would sit up to a banquet of chemicalized foods and get sick, while the poor would have nothing to eat at all. There is nothing in the Bible—Old or New Testament—which can get us out of the food crisis in which mankind now finds itself.

Simply to proclaim the freedom of the Christian to eat what he pleases is sheer suicide. To be sure, we are free from outmoded myths about food. But our new-won freedom in Christ must be used with reason. The gospel does not give us the freedom to do damage to ourselves and to others; we are not free to destroy the earth and the food it yields. Christian freedom must inform itself of the conditions under which it may act responsibly, concretely and for the human good. It cannot act in a vacuum or turn a saying of Jesus into a timeless principle.

We must forge a new link between Christian faith and food. We are, after all, in a new situation. Our food is being spoiled, we are becoming sick and the earth is being depleted, and everything will get worse without a revolution to change all that. We are certainly not proposing that we go back to the good old days. Nothing of that sort! Even less would we ask Christianity to revert to the legalism from which it broke in the first century. If any of the food laws in Judaism make sense today, that is their good luck. We would insist on modern nutritional reasons to observe them. Most remote of all, from our standpoint, is any thought of looking toward the East for ready-made answers. Admittedly, many people have found help in Zen macrobiotics and other Eastern philosophies which challenge traditional Western concepts of nutrition and medicine. Hardly anyone expects much help from Christianity. As the dominant religion of Western society it has failed to lift high the values dealing with the human body and the food of the earth. It has witnessed the general public going like lambs to the slaughterhouse of big food interests without yet making a loud complaint.

In the next decade food will become the chief concern of the human race. Not war and peace, not oil and energy, not communist and capitalist ideology, but food will be the number one issue. It will be the pacemaker of all the other factors deciding global harmony. Hence, the link between Christian faith and food must be a new one. The principles and platitudes of the past will not suffice. For this reason we do not believe that the other world religions now have the philosophies of food that will lead mankind out of the wilderness into a promised land flowing with milk and honey.

From Dust Unto Dust

The human body becomes concretely united with the earth through the food which is eaten. A favorite theme of Luther's theology was the "whole man." That has a peculiarly contemporary ring. We can hear its echoes in such modern slogans as "whole earth" and "whole foods." A concern for the whole person must include the food and the earth which get converted into the human body. We can say: the whole person has a God-given right to whole food from the whole earth. The human being cannot find whole food if the earth is halfway depleted of its best nutrient properties. The medieval schoolmen had a saying for it: *ex nihilo nihil fit*. Out of nothing you get nothing. The food will transmit to the body only the elements it takes from the earth—no more, no less.

Genesis says that we are part of the earth and the earth is part of us, "From dust thou art and unto dust shalt thou return" (Gen. 3:19). The Christian doctrine of creation has tended to neglect the earthly medium of human life. The human being is one of the vital forms of the earth, albeit the highest. Hence, the expression "mother earth." "Adama" is the Hebrew name for earth, whose first son is Adam, the Man. The earth is felt to be womb, home, and grave. So closely is human life bound to the earth, feeling its radical dependence, that some religions tend to deify the earth and its powers or to capitalize "Nature." A mystical harmony with the earth is sensed as the source and ground of bodily life. Ralph Waldo Emerson, for example, wrote: "The greatest delight which the fields and woods minister is the suggestion of an occult relation between Man and vegetable."[1]

Perhaps the food crisis will provide the occasion for Christian theology to overcome its much bemoaned prejudice against the natural. Christianity, it is widely believed, is interested more in supernatural things, like supernatural food and drink. Listen to Feuerbach: "With Christianity," he says, "man lost the capability of conceiving himself as a part of Nature, of the universe."[2] Certain dominant trends in Christianity have nourished a supernatural attitude that places man too high above the earth to care about such an everydayish thing as food, together with an antinatural attitude, which remains coldly indifferent to the brute technology that is raping the earth. The body-soul dualism that we dealt with in the first chapter reflects itself in a split between man and the earth, between the subjective spirit of man and the objective world outside.

In the biblical world the God of history is also the Lord of nature. The world is not split into two realms, soul against body, individual against society, and man against nature. To be sure, Jahweh as the God of history struggled against Baal, the god of fertility whom the Canaanites worshiped in their nature festivals. However, the prophets of Israel, in attacking the idolatry entailed in the religion of fertility, were in fact affirming the lordship of Jahweh over the earth and the entire natural order.

The grace of God does not so much shower his people with gifts of a supernatural kind, but rather gets involved in the sanctification of the natural. "Grace does not destroy but perfects nature," said Thomas Aquinas. He had primarily in mind *human* nature, but the saying is theologically true also for our whole natural environment.

In Israel's faith nature is also the creation of God with its own vitalities and functions. The festivals based on the seasonal rhythms of nature brought joy to the people. Like the Pilgrim Fathers in our own American history, they praised God for the good earth, its yield of grain and oil and fruit. Israel was liberated from the worship of earth, from cultic participation in the rituals of earth's renewal. Whatever the origins of the Westerner's alienation from nature, they do not rest on the traditions of Israel. Israel did not sever its connection with the earth. The promise by which she lived included hope for a good land flowing with milk and honey.[3]

Man Is What He Eats!

Nothing more concretizes a person's connection with the earth than the food he eats. The well-known saying of Ludwig Feuerbach makes the point: *Man ist was man isst.* We are what we eat. On the surface this smacks of materialistic reductionism. But let us take it in its plainest meaning. All the basic elements which make up the human body are found in the earth. The essential nutrients for life enter the human organism through the food it eats. By some chemical miracle earthly food becomes changed into human life. In addition to food, of course, the body requires air and water from the environment. Breathing and drinking are as necessary as eating.

The entire symbol system in the Bible and Christian faith is based on such natural functions as eating, drinking, and breathing. It is obscene that Christians should be numbered among those who do not care. They are without excuse, for they have been called to keep the temple of the Holy Spirit clean. It is imperative to demand real food, good food, out of reverence for the interior ecology of the body—the home of the Spirit. In the Bible we do not meet a metaphysics of food as in Oriental philosophy, with its theory about Yin and Yang; but we do find a symbolics of food. It is most concentrated in the sacrament of eating bread and drinking wine. Enigmatically Norman Brown says: "The question what is a body, is the question what is it to eat: Take, eat; this is my body."[4] The symbols and sacraments of faith become perverted if they are spiritualistically detached from the profane acts of eating and drinking. A theology of the body is concerned about the earth and the food it yields, because the message of salvation comes down to us in a sacrament of the flesh (Jesus), in a sacrament of water (baptism), in a sacrament of bread and wine (the meal of thanksgiving). All this should work to heighten our consciousness of the body and its foods for life. Literally, bread and wine become metabolized into flesh and blood. You really are what you eat!

In earlier Christian spirituality eating and drinking were in themselves religious acts. The simple act of offering a prayer before and after the meal gave a religious frame to eating and drinking. Family, food, and faith were all brought together in the same time and space. Compare that to the secular style in America today. People rush in from the streets, do not compose themselves through any ritual, gulp down some synthetic foods and disperse again as nervous as when they began.

When Feuerbach said, *"Der Mensch ist was er isst,"* he was asking philosophy to look at man concretely through the eyes of the new science of food chemistry. He accused philosophers, in their quest for truth, of having overlooked what was literally right under their noses. And theologians, frightened off by Feuerbach's denial of God, have used it as a pretext to ignore everything good he said. Consider this quotation:

> Eating and drinking is the mystery of the Lord's Supper;—eating and drinking is, in fact, in itself a religious act; at least, ought to be so. Think, therefore, with every morsel of bread which relieves thee from the pain of hunger, with every draught of wine which cheers thy heart, of the God who confers these beneficent gifts upon thee—think of man! But in thy gratitude towards man forget not gratitude towards holy Nature! Forget not that wine is the blood of plants, and flour the flesh of plants, which are sacrificed for thy well-being! Forget not that the plant typifies to thee the essence of Nature, which lovingly surrenders itself for thy enjoyment! Therefore forget not the gratitude which thou owest to the natural qualities of bread and wine! And if thou art inclined to smile that I call eating and drinking religious acts, because they are common everyday acts, and are therefore performed by multitudes without thought, without emotion; reflect, that the Lord's Supper is to multitudes a thoughtless, emotionless act, because it takes place often; and, for the sake of comprehending the religious significance of bread and wine, place thyself in a position where the daily act is unnaturally, violently interrupted. Hunger and thirst destroy not only the physical but also the mental and moral powers of man; they rob him of his humanity—of understanding, of consciousness. Oh! if thou shouldst ever experience want, how wouldst thou bless and praise the natural qualities of bread and wine, which restore to thee thy humanity, thy intellect! It needs only that the ordinary course of things be interrupted in order to vindicate to common things an uncommon significance, *to life, as such, a religious import.*

> Therefore let bread be sacred for us, let wine be sacred, and also let water be sacred! Amen.[5]

Such passages in Feuerbach's writings explain why he is one of our favorite heretics. He stressed as few others the *carni* of the incarnation, taking up—as he believed—the sacramental realism of Luther's notion that the body and blood of Christ are really present *in, with, and under* the bread and the wine. Feuerbach arrived on the scene when the new science of nutrition was in its infancy. As a convert he let himself get carried away into exaggerations and simplicities which now sound absurd. After reading a book by Moleschott on nutrition, *Lehre der Nahrungsmittel,* he thought he could explain all the great philosophical categories—substance, being, existence, essence, idea—in terms of the new revolutionary principles of food chemistry. To the exasperation of his fellow philosophers and theologians he now said,

> Everything depends upon what we eat and drink. Difference in essence is but difference in food. . . . How the philosophers have tortured themselves with the question as to where and with what philosophy begins. . . . Oh, you fools, who open your mouth in sheer wonder over the enigmas of the beginning and yet fail to see that the open mouth is the entrance to the heart of nature: who fail to see that your teeth have long ago cracked the nut upon which you are still breaking your heads. . . . But the beginning of existence is nourishment; therefore, food is the beginning of wisdom. The first condition of putting anything into your head and heart is to put something into your stomach.[6]

From this point Feuerbach goes on to make food the key to history. The workers in Europe don't have the energy for a revolution because they live on a potato diet. "Sluggish potato blood," said Feuerbach, spelled defeat for the Irish against the English, who had roast beef. Likewise, India with its vegetarian diet was chained to the chariot wheel of the British Empire. The hope for all oppressed people lies in a better diet. In a classic passage Feuerbach writes, "We see what important ethical significance the doctrine of food has for the people. What is eaten turns to blood, the blood to heart and brain, to the stuff of thought and temperament. Human fare is the foundation of human culture and disposition. Do you want to improve the people? Then instead of preaching against sin, give them better food. Man is what he eats."[7]

The science of nutrition has come a long way since Feuerbach in the mid-nineteenth century. Prior to his time ideas about diet had been dominated by the influence of Hippocrates, the Father of medicine. He taught that all foods contain more or less of the same stuff. He called it the "universal aliment." Eat enough of it, and you'll be all right. Heavier foods like meat and potatoes will fill you up faster with the universal aliment than, say, leafy green vegetables and fresh fruits. It's hard to believe, but that's the way people thought up to a century ago. As food chemists began to question the authority of Hippocrates, countering with the novel teaching that some foods supply one thing, others quite another, they were laughed at as food faddists and quacks. Just like today when the established opinions of doctors and scientists are challenged by new discoveries about foods and our health.

Many people still live in the dark ages when it comes to the foods they eat. They act as though the purpose of eating is "to get filled up." The first scientific step beyond Hippocrates did not bring much change for the better. We have in mind the invention of the calorie —a unit of measurement for the heat which food produces in the body.[8] Scientists discovered that some foods contain more calories than others, especially these loaded with starch, sugar, and fat. This led people to prefer foods high in calorie content. Calories produce heat and heat produces energy; energy means motion and life. So, people were led to reason, we need lots of that kind of food. Food manufacturers competed with each other to give the people what they wanted, especially new kinds of cereal. Again, many fruits and vegetables came in last place in the calorie race. Americans started on their diet of calories which is hard to shake. They are turning high calorie foods into heat and energy and storing them as fat.

Americans have become as a consequence undernourished and overweight.

Man cannot live on calories alone, especially the empty calories that make up a large part of the American diet. In the process of doing research in animal feeding, agricultural scientists discovered proteins, the chief substance in building up flesh and blood. The word *protein* comes from the Greek word *proteios* meaning "of prime importance." A person cannot live without it. Most of what you are is made of protein. For this reason we are not much impressed by orthodox vegetarianism which shuns all animal protein, our most available source of the complete protein our bodies need. To be sure, there are other sources of protein. But it seems unnatural and unnecessary for humans to narrow their protein sources down to some nuts and soybeans. That is a case of dogma flying in the face of science.

In addition to carbohydrates (sugar and starch) and proteins, our bodies need fats, minerals, vitamins, and water. Even overweight people must not try to get rid of all fats in their diet. The right amount keeps the skin clear and nerves calm. Fats give energy and insulation for the body tissues. But there are two kinds of fat; saturated fats are solid while unsaturated fats are liquid. Both are essential, but with all the scare about cholesterol many advise that we cut down on the hard fats and use polyunsaturated fats—easier to digest.

The average family has been led to believe that it is eating well on three square meals a day. Schools and professional medicine teach that we should eat a balanced diet. What they do not stress is that three square meals a day and a so-called balanced diet can be woefully deficient in essential minerals and vitamins. Animal experiments have shown that on a diet of pure carbohydrates, proteins, and fats, free of minerals, the animals died in a matter of weeks. On the same diet the animals lived significantly longer when minerals were added. Minerals in food are essential to human welfare. Where are they found? In fruits and vegetables. That's where they are *supposed* to be found. But you can't be sure. If the good earth has been robbed of its minerals, its produce will be mineral-poor. A vegetable can pass on to us only what it gets from the soil. And if the minerals are not recycled, the soil will become inferior and finally depleted.

Fruits and vegetables are also rich in vitamins. Around the turn of the century scientists were discovering that life cannot be sustained without vitamins. The same experiments which showed that animals died without minerals were showing that a protein-carbohydrate-fat-mineral diet was not enough. There must be additional food factors which contain the secret of life. They were called vitamins, because the prefix *vita* means life. At about the same time, around World War I, it was found that vitamin D (sunshine) could cure rickets, that vitamin B (the outer hull of rice) cured beriberi, and that vitamin C (lemon juice) cured scurvy. The march was on to discover other vitamins the lack of which was the cause of disease. This opened up a whole new approach to healing—the nutritional way. Diseases can be caused by vitamin deficiencies. You attack the disease not by fighting germs but by supplying the right vitamins. Disease is not only caused by the presence of some foreign bodies, but by the absence of some vital foods—vitamins.

The concept of a balanced diet is a sound one if we know what is in our foods. It is utterly stupid to believe that by filling up three times a day on supermarket foods, we can be assured of an all-around healthful diet. The chances are good that only a small number of people are now eating right. Perhaps many who read this book will not have the haziest idea of the nutritional merits of what they eat or where to begin to turn their diet around. Our people have been sold a diet damaging to health. What they have learned in school or at home or from the medical professionals has left them defenseless before the lies and deceptions of the big food industries. Their specialty is making money, not promoting health. One cannot learn the fundamental facts about foods and nutrition that lead to greater health and fuller life without making a studied effort to unlearn or at least question practically everything that has come to him through regular channels of information. He must find new and more credible sources of food knowledge as well as new and more reliable sources of wholesome food. In our society it is a narrow path; but the broad road leads to destruction. Read on!

Food Pollution

A homemaker stated before congressional hearings on food additives, "The shopper, really informed and looking for a plain food with nothing added or taken away, is like Diogenes with a lantern unable to find an honest man."[9]

The story begins down on the farm. Or even before that—in the chemistry laboratory. For the first time in human history a whole generation is feeding itself on chemicalized food. Farmers naturally want bigger crops and higher prices with less work and risk. So they are all ears when a chemical salesman comes along to promise these things. As it turns out there is hardly a tomato or an apple to be had anywhere which has not been doctored with chemicals from seedtime to harvest. Sure, they look good, all the same size and color, but inside and out there are ingredients hazardous to human health, and in addition they are almost tasteless. Many Americans have never eaten organically grown fruits and vegetables and so do not know what plain natural foods are supposed to taste like. Eye appeal, not taste appeal, money making and not health creating, shelf life, not human life—these are the upside-down values which the food business is ramming down the throats of the consuming public.

The sad truth is that poisons are polluting our food and therefore us—our bodies. A poison is a poison, and no one has a moral right to put it in our food for any reason whatsoever. The quality of the food is declining with continued use of artificial fertilizers. Long time use of chemical fertilizers unbalances the soil, decreasing the nutrient value of the food. While nitrogen, phosphorous, and potash are generously applied for quick growth, the soil becomes deficient in other elements important for health-giving food. And the food becomes excessively doped with nitrates, causing nitrate poisoning. Fruits and vegetables are doused with insecticides, pesticides, weedicides, leaving residues that permeate the cellular structure of the plants. There's no way to get rid of the chemicals by soaking, washing, or cutting away the peelings.

Our fruits and vegetables are picked way before they are ripe, so they can be stored a long time and shipped to far away places. They look so lush in their cellophane wrapping, don't they? But all that glitters is not gold. The fresh fruit look that you see is all an illusion; the chances are that they have been gassed or oiled or waxed or subjected to some chemical treatment which consumers have never been told about. Green citrus fruit is painted the right color. Oranges, as everyone knows who's peeled one, are artificially colored. The dye is known to be cancer-causing in mice. Oranges should be labeled "poisonous." If consumers still want to eat them, let them have their way. But the deception that we permit the food industry, with the okay of our government's Food and Drug Administration (FDA), is making fools of us and victims of poison. The story is endless, once we permit such tampering with food in the first place. Dried fruits? They, like many other foods, are given the sulphur dioxide treatment. Sprayed, dusted, fumigated with your favorite chemicals—you're getting more than you bargained for. The basic premise is: what people don't know won't hurt them.

To go from bad to worse, we have reluctantly reached the conclusion that most meat in this country is unfit for human consumption. Reluctantly, we say, because meat is the best source of protein and, besides, we like it. But the more we learn the less we can eat of commercial beef. First of all, the land on which livestock has been raised has been rendered deficient by synthetic fertilizers. William Albrecht, a soil scientist, quipped that the grass *is* greener on the other side of the fence. The cow is not trying to be naughty, but in its wisdom is only seeking to move away from the empty grass grown on worn-out soil. Secondly, shortly before slaughter the animals are taken to feedlots and fattened as quickly and cheaply as possible. Thirdly, the chief fattening agent is a drug known to cause cancer in animals. This is diethylstilbestrol, sometimes referred to as DES or simply stilbestrol. It is a synthetic estrogenic hormone used widely in the United States but banned in most of the other major cattle-producing countries. Fourthly, the consumer is getting shortchanged because he is paying protein prices for filthy fat.

No one knows how much stilbestrol it takes to cause cancer in a human being. But we do know that Americans eat lots of meat and that cancer is on the rise. Furthermore, cancer experts tell us that "no amount or dosage of a substance known to be cancer-inciting in animals can be presumed safe for man."[10] The FDA has the responsibility to safeguard the health of the American people, but because of the "politics of meat"[11] it, together with the U.S. Department of Agriculture, continue to dance around the golden calf.

In addition to stilbestrol, animals and fowl are given numerous other drugs, in the form of antibiotics and tranquilizers. The drug residues find their way into our bodies. None of the meat escapes the drug treatment centers: pork, veal, lamb, chicken, turkey, etc. All of it is more or less polluted. Finally, even the fish and all water life are exposed to poisons, the degree of contamination depending on how close the fish live to human civilization. One has to know where the seafoods come from to be sure they are quite safe.

Give Us Our Daily Bread

"White bread is a wholesome, nutritious food," says an official of the American Medical Association. Against this there's an old Scot saying, "The whiter the bread, the sooner you're dead." Who's right? Bread is more than something to eat. It is a symbol—a central religious symbol of the Bible; in later times a class symbol —dark bread for the poor people and white bread for the rich; at the present time it is a symbol of world power, actually a club in the hands of the rich nations to make the hungry ones knuckle under. Bread is an effective weapon in the arsenal of food-exporting nations.

Christians ought to know something about bread. It is one of the seven petitions of the Lord's Prayer: "Give us this day our daily bread." Bread and faith are intertwined in the Bible: If this connection is lost to us, perhaps we would better understand if we say that bread and peace (another biblical symbol) are necessarily linked in the modern world. Either bread and peace, or hunger and war. The revolutionary struggle in the world boils down to each man wanting to get his hand firmly planted on the bread knife. But now, this most precious symbol of life—the very staff of life—has become so devitalized, literally devitaminized, that it loses much of its value as food. It has become difficult to think of a loaf of white bread as a symbol of real life. It has been referred to as "presliced absorbent cotton," "cotton fluff wrapped up in a skin," "as appetizing as white foam rubber without the spring and the bounce."[12]

Alan Watts writes about the all-American loaf as "a vitamin-enriched styrofoam," "a virtually weightless compound of squishy and porous pith injected with preservatives and allegedly nutritive chemicals. It is not so much white as ideally and perfectly colorless, and approximates as nearly as human genius can manage to the taste of absolute nothingness. It is a compact of air bubbles each contained in a film of edible plastic which has been synthesized from wheat or rye as one gets casein from milk. In contact with liquid, be it gravy or saliva, this plastic film disintegrates at once into a cloying and textureless paste exactly like the revolting white slime which is fed to babies, and which most babies, quite understandably, spit back into the spoon."[13]

On closer analysis, the story of the fall of bread in our culture is bound up with the original sin of a dehumanizing technology and capitalistic economics. It is impossible for the bread business to get rich on healthy bread. Capitalism cannot make as much money on a good loaf of bread. There's the demand for huge profits and for long shelf-life, so that chemical preservatives have to be added. Refined white flour is used, accomplishing two things: aesthetically the whiteness poses as a symbol of what's clean and pure, and nutritionally, the germs of life have been extracted so that, notoriously, not even the bugs can live in it. Nothing better illustrates the "dietetic promiscuity" into which the food industry has lured the American people than what has happened to a loaf of bread. Writing in *The Commune Cookbook* a young author of recipes states: "Baking a loaf of brown bread in this society is revolutionary, if you know why you're doing it. It is for us. It also tastes good and helps keep you well."[14]

There are two things wrong with the white flour which goes into our bread, doughnuts, sweet rolls, pies, cakes, cookies, and cereals. A lot of the good things have been taken out—the valuable nutrients—and chemicals have been put in their place. The whitening of the whole grain means removing the bran and the germs of the wheat. These are fed to animals and people who shop in health food stores. The American horse, someone has said, has a better diet than the American people. Then, too, bread is bathed in chemicals all the way from the soil to the kitchen. Starting with artificial fertilizers and insecticides on the farm, the wheat is treated with a chemical to keep it from spoiling, then others to bleach, age, and sterilize it, still others to serve as dough conditioners, softeners and emulsifiers, and finally preservatives and stale-inhibitors.

The greatest insult to the American consumer is the advertising of "enriched" bread. The impression is given that we are getting all that nature offers, plus some extra enrichment to make us healthy. The truth is that enrichment is an attempt to put back into the bread some of what has been extracted through the milling process. But the term is a joke, for usually only three synthetic vitamins (thiamin, riboflavin, and niacin) and one mineral (iron), are added after a long list of vitamins and minerals, essential for radiant health, has been removed. The end product is a worthless food.

Eating, American Style

"What man of you, if his son asks him for a loaf, will give him a stone? Or if he asks for a fish will give him a serpent?" (Matt. 7:9–10). The context has changed. Who among us, if our children ask us for treats, do not give them a dollar for pop and potato chips, candy and ice cream, TV dinners and Hostess Twinkies and other kinds of cellophane wrapped junk? There's a myth going around that America is the best-fed nation in the world. But actually, from a nutritional viewpoint, we have gone a long way down hill. With so much food around and going to waste, Americans believe that whatever their problems are, they can't be caused by lack of food. But food is not nutrition. Over half of the boys in the last draft had to be rejected, not for lack of food but for defects caused by poor nutrition. Teenagers are growing up on candy bars and soft drinks loaded with sugar and carbon dioxide gas. They start out with a breakfast of sugar-soaked cereals, for lunch they have a bleached sandwich, and for dinner a frozen meal embalmed in chemicals. That is all food—junk food; not an ounce of it can be called nutritious.

The whitening of food is a chief cause of the malnutrition built into the American food economy. Over two-thirds of our food calories are coming from devitalized processed foods such as white flour, white sugar, and white rice. Sugar is the sweetest demon of all. If it is brown, forget it. The brown coloring usually comes not from the molasses but from the bone-charcoal treatment. That fooled us too for quite a while. Now we have no sugar in the house, and we avoid all foods as much as possible to which refined sugar has been added. For sweetening we use honey—an excellent food if you get it raw, unfiltered, and unheated. Otherwise it may not be natural, made by honey bees from flower blossoms. One thing is sure—we can get along without adding sugar to anything. If only there would be a sugar crisis in the world, we might upgrade the American diet by getting along with less of our most unneeded food. Starting with breakfast, who needs nature's juices to be sweetened? Who needs to add sugar to already sweetened cereals? Who needs sugar syrup rather than *pure* honey or *pure* maple syrup, for waffles and pancakes already loaded with empty calories from white flour and white sugar? Who needs sweet quick-energy snacks at every coffee break? Who needs the sugary desserts that are rotting our teeth and disturbing our blood sugar? The average American consumes between one and two hundred pounds of sugar a year, and going along with this statistic is a rapid increase in degenerative diseases.

Americans are always in a hurry. More and more they are taking to ready-made foods. The trade calls them "convenience foods." The head of the FDA said in a recent interview that by 1980 about two-thirds of the meals on the American dinner tables will have been prepared outside the home. People are buying more prepackaged and processed foods. This means that much of our grocery money is going for nonfood factors, like chemicals and packages and the million-dollar advertising campaigns to fool the public through misrepresentation and mislabeling. Food technologists have succeeded in making synthetic food and drinks, tasteless and nutritionally minus, but very expensive.

Eating out is not what it used to be. The quality of food in restaurants has been getting inferior. The food is flat, badly cooked, low in nutrient value, and dangerous to eat. Seldom can you find a restaurant which builds a meal from basic foodstuffs. The foods are prepared ahead of time elsewhere, shipped frozen and served to the unwitting customer as fresh. Highway dining is getting so bad we have to bring along our own food. *The New York Times* bemoaned "the plastic hamburger, the asbestos French fry, apple mucilage pie, peas and limas plucked back in the Eisenhower years, and cardboard bread, all brought back from beyond the grave through the miracle of food freezing. From Secaucus to Key West, 'half southern fried chicken' is available in brown, glove-like rubber casings of the chicken. 'Seafood platters' come similarly packaged in rubber batter; unpackaged, the shrimp taste like scallops, which taste like the flounder, which taste like catsup."[15] As we see motorists pile in and out of these restaurants we wonder if people have forgotten what real food properly prepared and served tastes like.

Institutional food is almost invariably a nutritionist's nightmare. School lunch programs, college and seminary cafeterias, and worst of all, the hospital menu are almost always serving up a feast of chemicals. The food is overcooked, the vitamins and minerals have been drained away, and what is left is a soggy pulp that tastes bad. Someone working in a modern hospital noted: "White bread, packaged cereals, canned foods predominate on the menus. Vegetables, when fresh, are boiled and reboiled. Salads are at a minimum."[16] Hospital patients should have the best food to speed their recovery. Doctors ought to pay more attention to what the sick are served. If only they knew as much about food as they know about drugs, as much about health as illness, the patients would get a diet commensurate with the $100-a-day fee for staying in the hospital.

There are families who cannot afford to eat the tasteless foods in restaurants or the foodless foods that have been all but predigested in supermarkets. They are trying to cook the old-fashioned way; it's cheaper and more healthful. It is not their intention to be eating plastic foods and other adulterated products. Plain food, plenty of it, tasty and a good variety, that's what they want. Trustworthy souls that they are, they do not know they are not getting plain foods from the earth. They do not know—no one has told them—that their foods have been shot through with chemicals and the way they have been processed has deprived them of their vitamin-mineral content. Finally, they put their own hands on the food and unwittingly apply the *coup de grace*. Someone has called it "murder in the kitchen." With tender loving care and old-fashioned methods the food is cooked to death, with more than half of the vitamins and minerals lost in the process. But the calories remain.

It is not enough to buy good food; it must be prepared right. We do not say "cooked" right, because as much as half of our diet should consist of raw foods. The unforgivable sin is to overpeel and overcook a vegetable, to use lots of water and pour it, along with the minerals and vitamins, down the drain. A balanced diet without proper cooking is impossible to achieve. Since the average person eats 150,000 pounds of food in a lifetime, it would seem most worthwhile to learn about its great potential for our weal or woe—how to grow or buy and cook and eat it.

In Search of Natural Foods

A love for food is the proper extension of love for one's own body and another's. No-body lives without eating. It is doing what comes naturally. But what are our chances of natural living in an artificial society? Technology has been able to conquer outer space. The inner space reserved for the foods of the earth has become a dumping ground of synthetic foods and chemical additives, insecticides, preservatives, stabilizers, colorings, and whatnot. Nature provides the body with all the materials necessary for vigorous health. If the chemist's help is needed, let us admit that it is because in modern urban living it is next to impossible to eat a balanced diet consisting entirely of organic natural foods. It is best to get our vitamins, minerals, proteins, and enzymes from meats, grains, nuts, fruits, and vegetables, etc., but if we are not succeeding at that, we are wise to use food supplements. That is where we need the chemist, not to mix harmful chemicals into our food, but to make supplements from natural sources to prevent malnutrition and disease. We are not opposed to the use of technology, only that it be used primarily for human health and not industrial wealth.

We have decided that when we sit up to a meal we do not want to eat hydrogen peroxide, sodium nitrate, diacetyl, calcium propionate, sodium phosphate, potassium bisulfite, magnesium sulfate, sodium carbonate and such things unnatural to foods. Yet these are only a few that we get in meat and cheese, butter and milk. On picnics we used to eat a concoction of muscle meat, pork stomach, unskinned pork jowls, pork salivary glands, lymph nodes and cheek fat, pork spleens, isolated soy protein, sodium erythorbate, sodium nitrate, sodium nitrite, and artificial coloring, in short, everything but "the pig's squeal and the cow's moo."[17] And we loved 'em. They're called hot dogs.

Once we commit ourselves to eating natural and nutritious foods, our options are drastically changed. We try, first of all, to buy foods grown in an organic way. For grains, fruits, and vegetables this simply means without artificial fertilizers, chemical sprays, and the like. As for meat, only a tiny fraction of the animals slaughtered in this country has been raised in a natural environment. However, there are a few suppliers and the search pays off in superior meat foods. Secondly, we try to use unprocessed foods. When the foods are processed we make sure that no artificial chemicals have been added and that the vital nutrients have not been lost. Especially the whitened foods are taboo. We found that by cutting out white sugar and all white flour products we had taken a giant step towards a more wholesome diet. Thirdly, our shopping loyalties gradually shifted from the supermarket to the natural food store. If enough people would do likewise, supermarkets would be forced to offer people a choice between synthetic-chemical and natural-organic foods.

What we hope for in the long run is a fundamental change in the system which finds it so profitable to feed people polluted food. The inner ecology of the body is linked to all the major environmental issues. The ecological fight must be fought on many fronts. But we believe a person will fight best when he begins at home—in his kitchen. It is foolish to wait for a big revolution out there, and neglect the one that concerns one's daily bread and personal health. We can't wait for ideal social, political, and economic structures to arrive. If a person feels the need to change, he can begin with his body as a whole, a complex and delicately balanced ecological system in itself. There is still time to make a choice in favor of quality food, chemically free and nutritionally rich. "For no one ever hated his own body: on the contrary he provides and cares for it" (Eph. 5:29).

NOTES

1. Quoted in *Cooking for Life*, by Michael Abehsera (Binghamton, N.Y.: Swan House, 1970), p. 11.
2. Ludwig Feuerbach, *The Essence of Christianity*, trans. George Eliot (New York: Harper & Row, 1957), p. 133.
3. See Walter Harrelson's study, *From Fertility Cult to Worship* (Garden City, N.Y.: Doubleday & Co., 1970).
4. Norman Brown, *Love's Body* (New York: Random House, Inc., 1966), p. 165.
5. Feuerbach, *The Essence*, p. 278.
6. Feuerbach, *Sämmtliche Werke*, 2nd ed., vol. 2, pp. 82, 83.
7. Ibid., p. 90.
8. One calorie has enough energy to raise one gram of water one degree centigrade.
9. Beatrice Trum Hunter, *Consumer Beware!* (New York: Simon and Schuster, 1971), p. 13.
10. *Food and Your Health*, ed. Beatrice Trum Hunter (New Canaan, Conn.: Keats Publishing, Inc., 1974), p. 35.
11. See *Sowing the Wind*, by Harrison Wellford, introd. Ralph Nader (New York: Grossman Publishers, 1972).
12. Hunter, *Consumer Beware!* p. 286.
13. Alan Watts, *Does It Matter?* (New York: Vintage Books, 1968), p. 30.
14. Crescent Dragonwagon, *The Commune Cookbook* (New York: Simon and Schuster, 1971), p. 129.
15. Hunter, *Consumer Beware!* pp. 64–65.
16. Ibid., p. 66.
17. Michael F. Jacobson, *Eater's Digest, The Consumer's Factbook of Food Additives* (New York: Doubleday & Co., 1972), p. 209.

A SELECT BIBLIOGRAPHY

Clark, Linda. *Know Your Nutrition*. New Canaan, Conn.: Keats Publishing, Inc., 1973.

Davis, Adelle. *Let's Eat Right to Keep Fit.* New York: Harcourt, Brace, Jovanovich, Inc., 1954.

Fredericks, Carlton. *Nutrition: Your Key to Good Health.* North Hollywood, Calif.: London Press, 1964.

Hauser, Gayelord. *Treasury of Secrets.* Greenwich, Conn.: Fawcett Publications, Inc., 1951.

Hunter, Beatrice Trum. *Consumer Beware!* New York: Simon and Schuster, 1971.

———., ed. *Food and Your Health.* New Canaan, Conn.: Keats Publishing, Inc., 1974.

Jacobson, Michael F. *Eater's Digest.* Garden City, N.Y.: Doubleday and Co., 1972.

Lindlahr, Victor H. *You Are What You Eat.* New York: Lancer Books, Inc., 1972.

Pritzker, Wendy. *Natural Foods.* New York: Dafran House Publishers, 1971.

Rodale, Robert, ed. *The Basic Book of Organic Gardening.* New York: Rodale Press, 1971.

Rorty, James, and Norman, N. Philip. *Bio-Organics: Your Food and Your Health.* New York: Lancer Books, Inc., 1956.

Wade, Carlson. *Vitamins and Other Food Supplements and Your Health.* New Canaan, Conn.: Keats Publishing, Inc., 1972.

Wellford, Harrison. *Sowing the Wind.* New York: Grossman Publishers, 1971.

Winter, Ruth. *A Consumer's Dictionary of Food Additives.* New York: Crown Publishers, Inc., 1972.

IV: Earth Imperatives

Whole Earth Theology

"The earth is the Lord's and the fulness thereof, the world and those who dwell therein" (Ps. 24:1). But we in the twentieth century have taken over the earth and turned it into a bloody battlefield. Technology has given us the tools to spoil the earth. The earth is suddenly becoming old and sick. Because the future of humanity is linked with the earth's we are now talking no longer about progress and a better world but about human survival and "lifeboat ethics."[1]

Much of the Western drama has been played out as the story of man's conquest over nature. When men climbed Mt. Everest they spoke of conquering it; when they went to the moon they boasted about conquering space. Modern man has placed a great strain on the earth, and the earth is crying out in pain. With technology as his club, man has been beating the earth as though it were something he hated. *The Environmental Handbook* offers this parable: "It is the top of the ninth inning. Man, always a threat at the plate, has been hitting Nature hard. It is important to remember, however, that NATURE BATS LAST."[2]

The earth will tolerate only so much of our civilized madness. After that a process could set in to rid the earth of its human enemies. It has happened before that when a species lives beyond its means, it suffers what is called "dieback." The species literally dies back to a level which its ecological milieu can afford. The same thing can happen to humanity if it continues on a collision course with the earth. An alternative must be charted. The Sermon on the Mount says, "Blessed are the meek, for they shall inherit the earth" (Matt. 5:5). The earth will be kind to creatures which show a certain meekness. Those who ignore its limits will go the way of the dinosaur. The dinosaur is a symbol of the creature that became "too big for its britches"—out of balance with its total environment.

Humanity is confronting the greatest crisis in its history. It is not the case that science and technology have failed us, as some would say. We have failed them, by asking them to be our gods and not our tools. We are encountering a deep failure of vision and will. This is where the Christian message is relevant. Science and technology cannot generate a vision and will of their own. The survival of mankind depends on the discovery of new dimensions of the human potential grounded in a holistic and global vision of man's symbiotic connections with the earth. Science and technology cannot themselves mount an attack on the evils of wasteful living, conspicuous consumption, manipulative advertising, growth for its own sake, poverty in the midst of plenty, water, air, and food pollution, overpopulation and military aggressiveness. Only the right religious vision can give us the earth imperatives to reverse the hell-bent course of things today.

There is nothing in the Christian message that ties us fatalistically to the barbarism that Western civilization is inflicting on humanity and the earth in the name of technological progress and economic growth. In the Christian vision the health of the whole person and the whole earth are linked to each other. There is no life and salvation apart from the whole body and the whole earth, whether now or in the lasting future of God. Salvation and healing must not be driven into separate spheres, one for religion and the other for medicine.

The body is the barometer of the state of the earth. The organs of the body send forth signals when the earth is poisoned, food is polluted, diseases begin to gallop and our medical services merely chase after symptoms. To be in touch with our bodies means being down to earth. Modern man is becoming a stranger to his own body because he has estranged himself from the earth around him. He has enveloped himself in a plastic culture and puts dead food into his mouth. No wonder that he is becoming numb. The channels of his body are getting clogged by the filth that is poured into the earth. The body finally becomes the dumping ground of poisonous air, chemicalized foods, and polluted water.

We are to our individual bodies what the whole body of mankind is to the earth. Our attitudes regarding our bodies reflect and express the way we look at the world around us. It is downright silly, for example, to fight for clean air in the city and then suck cigarette smoke into our lungs. We must learn that we are dovetailed into the world. We simply die without day-to-day communion with the vital systems of the good earth. Good body ecology is the key to the renewal of the earth on a global scale.

Christianity has received lots of blame for our present ecological predicament. Just as Gnostic Christianity showed a contempt for the body, so Western Christianity has exhibited an arrogance over against nature. Sometimes with savage ruthlessness Christians have heeded the biblical command to have dominion over the earth. They have stood by, many of them, watching the destruction of the earth in the interest of capitalistic enterprises. Capitalism is a system, as its record shows, of securing gold for some but garbage for everyone. "The love of money is the root of all evil" (I Tim. 6:10) the Bible says. It is doubtful that we will gain control of the means to heal the environment until we put big business out of business. All the profits of the big corporations to date have been gained at the expense of the Lord's earth, which he gave to his people as a garden to be dressed and cared for.

Critics of Christianity are looking elsewhere for sources of ecological renewal. Pantheism in particular seems to offer new hope. Pantheism holds that we ought to care for the earth because its life is at one with the very life of God. All living things are sacred. Albert Schweitzer's idea of "reverence for life" has sparked a new interest in vegetarianism, sometimes coupled with a refusal to use animal products of any kind. Some believe that by redivinizing all things, people will show a softer attitude toward nature. The trouble with this view is that it works only for those who are so religiously motivated. It not only flies in the face of orthodox Christianity, which maintains a distinction between God and his creation, but also counts on more idealism than this secular world can muster.

People will have to be convinced that caring about the earth lies in their own self-interest. Not because Nature is God, not because the earth is personified as our mother or brother or sister, not because the Bible commands us to be stewards of the earth, but largely because of somatic self-interest will people and corporations develop a new policy toward the earth. There is in Christianity an anthropocentric viewpoint that comes from the Bible. We have no good reason to abandon it. Man is made in the image of God; he is placed in a superior position over the rest of nature, just a little lower than the angels. True, he can grossly abuse this privilege; he can become a brute, a rapist of the earth and a mad-dog killer in the animal kingdom. And he will go on being this way if he thinks he can get away with it. Nor has the appeal to posterity, concern for the coming generations, motivated people much to care for the life-support systems of the earth. What has posterity ever done for us?

Caring for the future is an ethical posture informed by a vision of the universal destiny and solidarity of all things, one which we share. But most people, and certainly large corporations, are persuaded first and foremost by what appeals to their self-interest. Caring for other creatures, for plants and animals and the entire earthly environment may be seen as an extension of a person's concern for his body. Ecology must be centered in the interest of the human body, or it will never command universal commitment. "For no one ever hated his own body: on the contrary, he provides and cares for it" (Eph. 5:29 NEB).

An ethic that begins with the enlightenment of the body, of course, needs to be supplemented by an ethical perspective that transcends self-interest. The power of love as revealed by God in Christ can direct a person beyond himself to seek the interest of others for their own sake, to care for the earth as a steward of God's creation and to celebrate its inherent beauty and goodness. However, the starting point and the common denominator of a general natural ethic that can persuade all people to work for environmental renewal is the fact that as the earth goes so goes the body. The totality of the body of the world is of interest to me because my own body is irrigated by whatever is running through it. That is the immediate implication of our condition as beings situated in the world.

The Black Horse of the Apocalypse

With our bodies we are bound to the earth and food is our umbilical cord. Once it is cut we are dead. Nothing makes us more aware of our dependence on the earth than when food is scarce. On Earth Day, April 22, 1970, our attention was focused on the environment, especially on pollution. Five years later the world food crisis was highlighted on Food Day—a more immediate problem. Food resources are not keeping up with the expanding population. Around a hundred and fifty years ago the world population passed the one-billion mark. It took over one hundred years to reach the second billion, thirty years to pass three billion, and only fifteen to reach four billion in 1975. This is called exponential growth. The best estimate is that the next billion will be produced in only ten years. By the end of the century the world's population will be double what it is now.

In the Revelation of St. John the seer tells about the Four Horsemen of the Apocalypse (6:1–8). Some people believe this vision relates to events at the end of history. The first horse is white and stands for conquest, the second is the red horse of war, and the third is the black horse of famine. The fourth is a pale horse and its rider's name is Death. Conquest, war, famine, and death—these are running like wild horses in history right now, whatever their reference to the future might be. One does not have to be skilled in prophecy to announce that we are entering an Age of Famine such as the earth has never seen. The coming great famines will be accompanied by terrifying riots. Hunger and anger go hand in hand. "They will pass through the land," it says in Isaiah, "grealy distressed and hungry; and when they are hungry, they will be enraged and will curse their king and their God" (Isa. 8:21). Can anyone blame them? How many millions of people will have to die before we reach an equilibrium between population limits and food resources? The World Food Conference in Rome late in 1974 played the fiddle of ideological politics while flames of large-scale starvation were threatening to engulf the masses.

In the United States we like to go from the one cause to another without making any fundamental changes. Under President Johnson we all sang, "We Shall Overcome," believing that we could win the war on poverty and gain racial justice. Under President Nixon we all joined the campaign to "Clean Up America" and cheered on Nader's Raiders. Earth Day ... ecology ... the environmental crisis ... peace in Vietnam: we were hopeful. After Watergate we entered a period of energy shortage, rising prices, and economic recession. At last the world food crisis! All of these problems are interconnected. There can be no piecemeal solutions, for these problems are systemic, structural, and linked to economic and political powers that are organized for their own advantages. Those that have the most want to keep it that way, even if it means destruction of the earth and deprivation of the poor. We have no doubt that the main drive to exploit the earth and the people who dwell therein stems from the original sin of self-indulgence. The whole econocentric system which we have created is erected on the acquisitive nature of the Old Adam in everyone of us. The Gross National Product reflects the production of ecologically destructive and wasteful products, at least half of which are totally unrelated to basic human needs. The United States represents 6 percent of the world's population and consumes around a third of the earth's nonrenewable resources. Right now every American lays claim to the grain resources of the world about sixteen times greater than that of the average Asian. Most of this is going into foods that titillate the palate but bloat the body into the shape of a blimp. It's not that Americans are more gullible than others, but they are manipulated by saturation advertising into becoming consumers of useless goods and harmful foods.

Let 'Em Eat Meat!

No solution to the world food crisis can be discussed in realistic or moral terms without finding a new way of eating. We have become a steak-oriented culture. In preparing a meal the first thing the average cook thinks about is meat. Everything else is built around it. Our highways are lined with steak houses and restaurant menus are weighted entirely on the side of meat choices. What's wrong with that? Isn't meat a good source of protein? Aren't we free to eat meat if we want?

If you became convinced that eating a pound of beef will deprive a starving world of twenty pounds of grain of equal protein value, could you eat it with a good conscience? Now that all the churches in America are concentrating on "Bread for the World," recommending hunger appeals, meatless Mondays and fasting, it will be necessary to translate these tokens of love into acts of justice based on some food facts.[3]

Fact 1. Half of our farmland is given to crops for animal feed.

Fact 2. Three-fourths of all our grain is fed to animals.

Fact 3. It takes around twenty pounds of grain protein to produce one pound of beef protein.

Fact 4. One acre of farmland can produce five times more protein in the production of cereals than by raising cattle.

Fact 5. Fish, a good protein source, is fed to livestock—half of the world's fish catch in 1968.

Fact 6. In the United States we are eating twice as much beef per capita as we did a generation ago. Of meat and poultry we eat 212 pounds a person every year.

When the peasants of France stormed the Queen's Palace she asked one of her aides, "What do the people want?" When told they have no bread, she responded, "Let them eat cake." This is the kind of response the American food industry is making to a starving world. While millions of people are dying for lack of grains, the United States' secretary of agriculture said, "Let 'em eat hamburger!" After returning from the World Food Conference in Rome he said, "The American appetite for high-quality protein foods is not abating—nor will it. . . . Our taste buds hunger for meat; they make sure we get enough."[4] Jesus' parable of Dives the rich man and Lazarus the poor man has become real history in the contrast between the rich nations gorging themselves on meat while millions of human beings are starving from protein deficiency.

Being our brother's keeper on a global scale must mean for each American a significant reduction of meat consumption. It does not mean going without meat altogether, but it requires more of us than a token sacrifice of one meat meal a week. A Harvard nutritionist has estimated that the amount of food 200 million Americans consume could feed one and a half billion people on a diet of the average Chinese person. We are not recommending that we bring our diet down to that level. We have a right to a healthful diet, no more and no less than other people of the earth. But the distance between a healthful diet and the grossly wasteful standard of American consumption leaves each of us a lot of room for change.

The first thing we must do as we become morally serious is to get to know our vegetables and grains once again. In the right balance they contain the protein we need. The second is to learn to cook in a way that is ecologically sound, nutritionally balanced and of high-protein quality, economically more reasonable and yet more tasty than by relying so much on meats. Thirdly, we would suggest boycotting meat from livestock that have been fed food fit for human beings. Cattle have the amazing ability to convert grass into protein. We should let them do so and then, if we want, eat the meat with a good conscience. Much of our land is good only for grazing. The fertile soil should be used exclusively for crops that nourish human beings. We need a new set of Ten Commandments to deal with the politics and economics of food on a global scale. Even our dogs are better fed than the majority of people in the world. "Is not this the fast that I choose . . . to share your bread with the hungry?" (Isa. 58:6–7). And, "If a brother or sister is ill-clad and in lack of daily food, and one of you says to them, 'Go in peace, be warmed and filled,' without giving them the things needed for the body, what does it profit?" (James 2:15–16).

The Green Revolution Turning Brown

In 1968 we heaved a sigh of relief when the first glowing reports of the "Green Revolution" were broadcast. Agricultural research had developed high-yield strains of wheat and rice. In many developing countries the results of the new seeds were spectacular. Expectations were soaring that the great famines could be averted. But now again things are looking bleak. The Green Revolution is turning brown.

The failure of the Green Revolution is due largely to costly technological boosters with a boomerang effect. The miracle seeds were deliberately bred for large fertilizer and pesticide inputs. The fertilizers are produced from petroleum products, at prices now out of reach to many developing countries. The Green Revolution is costly and available primarily to those with the capital to invest. The big landholders swallow up the land of the small farmers. Social disruption ensues. One tractor can put a thousand people out of work under the conditions of traditional Asian agriculture. The West is exporting a revolution that is, furthermore, proving to be ecologically disastrous in the long run. The chemicals in fertilizers and pesticides get into the food and water, into milk and meat, and finally lodge in the human body. It is also possible that such chemical intervention will produce a new breed of pest, wiping out large areas.

Agricultural research and technology can play a part in the developing countries, but they have to be adapted to local economic and social conditions. The American model won't work in most places. The incentive that makes our farmers work hard is to cash in on big profits from high prices. But as it benefits them it puts the food out of reach of the poor people. Something as important as food for human survival should not be in the hands of a few land capitalists. The earth is the Lord's. It should serve all his people and not exist primarily for profits.

Transcending Hope

The deeper we get into the field of ecology the more gloomy we become about the future of mankind. Those who dismiss the ecological problems of population, pollution, energy and food shorages as mere "housekeeping details" are part of the problem. Oftentimes they take a fast retreat into religion and use it as an opiate for their headaches. That is exactly what the big profit-making corporations want us to do. It removes the pressure from government and business to do something commensurate with the magnitude of the problems we face. Ecology requirements are relaxed as soon as corporation profits are being squeezed.

On the other hand, we must stand fast in face of the doom-peddlers who would make us panic and lose our heads. We are being told in no uncertain terms that the earth is too small a spaceship to accommodate everybody on board. Some will have to be sacrificed. The weaker ones will have to be shoved overboard to leave enough room for the rest of us. We must choose who shall die, who is not worthy to live, who does not measure up to our definition of what it means to be a useful human being. The cheap killings in Vietnam and Cambodia, the starving millions in the Sahel and Bangladesh, and the masses of unborn babies who die in abortion have made us so morally groggy and insensitive to life that fiendish proposals are calmly debated by future scientists. One such is the much discussed "lifeboat ethics" advanced by Professor Garrett Hardin, in "The Case Against the Poor."[5] Hardin pictures the world situation today as one in which the rich nations of the world are in a few lifeboats and the poor nations are swimming around trying to get on board. There is not enough room in the boats for everyone and not enough provisions to share with the masses. If anyone motivated by guilt or compassion wishes to jump overboard and give his place to another, he should be free to do so. But that is not an obligation he can place on all the rest. Translated into policy this means—if our own native drive to survive is healthy—that we on board will take a realistic attitude of "benign neglect" to all those hopeless ones adrift at sea. To share what we have would spread it too thin and invite catastrophe for everyone. Most of all it would greatly inconvenience those of us who are comfortably seated in our lifeboats.

Such a picture lays all the burden on the population issue and deflects our attention from the fact that the affluence of the rich countries places a far greater stress on the earth's carrying capacity. Rising population is the problem of many—but not all—of the underdeveloped countries, but rising affluence in the wealthy countries is gobbling up energy and food far out of proportion to their needs or numbers. If the people in the lifeboats are consuming provisions that belong to the drowning masses, then it is our Christian ethical duty to rock the boats. We must begin radically to question our lifestyle of affluence, waste, destructiveness, the pursuit of money, and the exploitation of the poor. The option of "lifeboat ethics" has to be flatly rejected in favor of an ethic that values every body as one's own. The starting point for an ethical scenario cannot be the split between the rich who now have it made and the poor who are trying to climb on board. That split in the human race has to be overcome by a vision of the ultimate unification of mankind on this small and finite planet. We must call for new earth imperatives that can promise to sustain all of its inhabitants in a system of just and free relationships.

Interdependence, not a new declaration of independence, is the only way forward for the whole of civilization and all its member nations. The United States, one of the giants, will find a formula of survival with others, or not at all. We have no moral right to an affluent future by ourselves, or in a select company of rich nations against the poor. We are now living it up as a prodigal nation, squandering resources unconscionably. It may take an unspeakable catastrophe to make us come to our senses. A time of judgment may be upon us, preceding the dawning of a new day for mankind.

Christian faith can minister to our need to find a new lifestyle in line with the earth's limited resources and the needs of the world's peoples. In the past we have defined our humanity in terms of an everexpanding concept of development. In economics we have expressed the drive toward transcendence on the model of growth. We grow or we die. The idea that there are limits to growth seemingly stabs at the heart of our American way of life. We instinctively reject a static future, an equilibrium society. But perhaps we have become hung up on a false concept of human transcendence. Transcendence may mean something else than growing bigger, getting richer, owning more, beating others, conquering space and winning at games that can be measured in purely quantitative terms. The god of GNP may be demythologized into meaning "Going No Place." We may accept the limits of our human and earthly finitude and still live transcendently toward an infinite horizon of meaning. This is what it means to believe in God as a fulfilling presence within the limits of our human condition.

If we can learn a new meaning of transcendence, we may drastically change our consumer-oriented lifestyle. Transcendence can mean to place a higher premium on the quality of life, less on the standard of living. Transcendence redefined can mean to use power to build up the earth and not as a naked instrument of domination. Transcendence can mean looking beyond technological solutions to problems which in fact arise out of an inner distortion of the human spirit. Transcendence can mean to live by symbols of hope when the times become evil and lead to heartbreak. It is the social function of faith to mediate the possibilities of transcendence no matter how grim the forecasts.

As people who live by hope, in spite of everything, we cannot stand by and witness the human race go like the Gadarene swine headlong over the abyss to its destruction. Even though the crises of today become the catastrophes of tomorrow, we are called to a mission of hope, to bring consolation to the suffering and courage to those who struggle to make a better world. Where there is hope, there is faith in new possibilities of transcendence that God is still releasing into our common life. Hope generates actions. Trends can change. Things can be different for humanity. The politics and economics of the United States that we know will not survive, but the earth on which our part of God's universal history is taking place can become new like a garden. And men and women, children and animals, birds and insects, flowers and trees, and all living things can find a new harmony and live at peace with each other in accordance with God's creative design. How we get from here to there in terms of policies and programs, in terms of new technology and institutions, is the most urgent question now facing the world.

NOTES

1. See the discussion below.
2. *The Environmental Handbook*, ed. Garrett De Bell (New York: Ballantine Books, Inc., 1970), p. 176.
3. The following facts, and many more, are available in *Diet for a Small Planet*, by Frances Moore Lappé (New York: Ballantine Books, 1971), pp. 3–30.
4. *Los Angeles Times*, editorial pages, 21 February, 1975.
5. Garrett Hardin, "The Case Against the Poor," *Psychology Today* 8, no. 4, September 1974.

A SELECT BIBLIOGRAPHY

Braaten, Carl E. "Toward an Ecological Theology," *Christ and Counter-Christ*, chap. 8. Philadelphia: Fortress Press, 1972.

———. "Caring for the Future: Where Ethics and Ecology Meet," *Eschatology and Ethics*, chap. 12. Minneapolis: Augsburg Publishing House, 1974.

Brown, Lester R. *In the Human Interest*. New York: W. W. Norton & Co., 1974.

De Bell, Garrett, ed. *The Environmental Handbook*. New York: Ballantine Books, 1970.

Dubos, René. *Man Adapting*. New Haven: Yale University Press, 1965.

Eco-Catastrophe. Editors of Ramparts. New York: Harper & Row, 1970.

Elder, Frederick. *Crisis in Eden*. Nashville, Tenn.: Abingdon Press, 1970.

Ewald, Ellen Buchman. *Recipes for a Small Planet*. New York: Ballantine Books, 1973.

Falk, Richard A. *This Endangered Planet*. New York: Random House, 1971.

Hamilton, Michael, ed. *This Little Planet*. New York: Charles Scribner's Sons, 1970.

Lappé, Frances Moore. *Diet for a Small Planet*. New York: Ballantine Books, 1971.

Meadows, Donnella H. et al. *The Limits to Growth*. New York: Universe Books, 1972.

Santmire, H. Paul. *Brother Earth*. New York: Thomas Nelson, Inc., 1970.

Sherrell, Richard E., ed. *Ecology, Crisis and New Vision*. Richmond, Va.: John Knox Press, 1971.

Strong, Maurice F., ed. *Who Speaks for Earth*. New York: W. W. Norton and Co., 1973.

Appendix I: Debunking Myths

Myth No. 1

That the American diet is a healthy one; in fact, it is the best in the world.

The American diet could be the healthiest in the world. There is no food known on earth that is unavailable to us. Yet, we rank among the highest in the consumption of empty calories, refined carbohydrates, and white sugar products. We rank high in consuming saturated and hydrogenated fats, high in eating processed and imitation foods rich in chemical preservatives and additives. Consumers are becoming sick on this food; yet they are dying to eat it.

Myth No. 2

That government agencies like the U.S. Department of Agriculture and the Food and Drug Administration can be trusted to make and enforce rules and regulations in the interest of the health of the consuming public.

These agencies have been created for consumer welfare, but the facts suggest that their decisions are often tailor-made to favor industry. They receive their "advice" from the trustees of industry in the drafting of legislation to "protect" the consumers from an overdose of chemicals in foods and cosmetics. Many of the faculty members of farm schools and universities who serve on government committees are also affiliated with the very businesses which government is to supervise. Consumer advocates who are most concerned about healthy unchemicalized foods unanimously report that USDA and FDA regularly bow to the pressures of agribusiness and pharmaceutical companies.

Myth No. 3

The American methods of food production are the only hope for the starving world. Where would the world be if it were not for the food we export?

America is in a strong position to help a hungry world, and many countries are in desperate need for our assistance. But America exports lots of nonessential foods, packaged products, corn flakes and potato chips, Coca-Cola and candy bars. Americans have an image of themselves as humanitarians. They do respond to a call for emergency relief. When Biafra was desperate a call went out from coast to coast for help. Three hundred tons of food were collected and shipped—breakfast cereals, vanilla puddings, cake mixes, Jello, cheese dips, ketchup, noodles, sweet pickles, and mustard. It was called "the pudding ship." The world does not need that kind of food.

Myth No. 4

That the common diseases Americans get—high blood pressure, varicose veins, hardening of the arteries, arthritis, ulcers, kidney stones, prostate gland trouble, colitis, senility, etc.—are all inevitably part of growing old.

Old people do not have to be ridden with a host of degenerative diseases. There is much evidence to show that people who nourish their cells and tissues with good nutrition and care for their bodies with proper sleep, recreation, and exercise can retain robust health throughout their life span. Heredity has much to do with *how long* a person lives, but good nutrition has a lot to say about *how well.*

Myth No. 5

People who are interested in health foods are quacks and faddists who believe there is a miracle cure for every disease.

As in every field there are false prophets who make promises they cannot back up. The only defense against charlatans is to be armed with knowledge and reliable information. People have jumped into the health food business purely for commercial reasons. Many of them have now gone bankrupt. The crackpots can be detected by the outlandish claims they make for a particular food or vitamin. There are no quickie cures the natural nutritional way. There is no single vitamin that can cure or prevent any disease. The truth is that by synergizing all the basic nutrients in a total program on a lifelong basis many diseases can be prevented or cured.

Myth No. 6

Natural foods cost too much for the average family. It is a luxury in which the upper-middle class indulges.

People who worry about low-income families spending too much money on natural foods should spare themselves this needless burden. The poor people are those who spend vast sums at the supermarket on candy, soft drinks, sweetened cereals, fluffy bread, cakes, ice cream, TV dinners, frozen foods, and the like. A person who eats right shops right, and that keeps the price of natural foods within reach of the average family. When one adds the cost of medical bills to the price of empty and poisoned foods people buy, natural foods are a bargain anyone can afford.

Myth No. 7

You get all the vitamins and minerals you need just by eating three square meals a day.

It is quite meaningless to talk about three square meals a day, considering what the modern shopper puts in his grocery basket. When a large part of the average meal is composed of sugar, white flour, and processed foods, there are bound to be nutritional deficiencies. Many of the original nutrients have been removed for "cosmetic" reasons, making the food look good but void of its vital elements. Considering all the chemicals we eat, the polluted environment and the stresses of modern day living, our bodies need all the help they can get from food supplements.

Myth No. 8

Too many vitamins and minerals can be dangerous to your health.

The Food and Drug Administration has been trying for quite a while to restrict the sale of vitamins. Pressure on government to control the intake of food supplements is coming from organized medicine and the food industry. A law that would make all vitamins in large doses available solely on the doctor's prescription would make him richer and do nothing for our health or pocketbook. The theory that vitamins in megadoses are dangerous is pure hypocrisy in a society in which all kinds of dangerous drugs in any quantity can be bought over the counter. The instances of people having taken too much of any vitamin are too rare to mention. How many people have taken too much aspirin, too many sleeping pills and amphetamines—people under doctor's care?

Myth No. 9

The amounts of chemicals in foods is so small that it won't hurt you.

No one knows what the safe level is for eating chemicals in foods that have been doused and bathed and colored and flavored by chemical preservatives and additives. No one knows the minimum you can ingest of poisonous substances like DDT, pesticides, weed-killers, and crop sprays without harmful effects on your body. There may be no safe level. Short-term effects may not be traceable; long-term effects catch up to you when it is too late. Since artificial chemical substances in your food do you no earthly good, why take a chance with them?

Myth No. 10

The sodium nitrite put in our hot dogs and cured meats is necessary and poses no danger to public health.

Many people who love the all-American hot dog have quit eating it when they found out about the hazards of sodium nitrite. Sodium nitrite can cause headaches and some people have died from nitrite poisoning in home-cured sausage. Most alarming, nitrites can combine with other chemicals (amines) in foods to form nitrosamines. Nitrosamines are known to be potent cancer-causing agents. Hot dogs and sausage products are available that are free of nitrite, proving that it is not necessary at all. Norway has banned the use of nitrite in hot dogs.

Appendix II: Food Supplements

The uninformed person has heard the propaganda that vitamin and mineral supplements are unnecessary. You get all you need by eating plain food. So why waste your money? We disagree. We are not living under normal conditions. We live far from Eden, in a polluted atmosphere and are deluged with foods that have been grown under poisoned conditions and processed by unnatural methods. Ideally we should be able to get all of the vital nutrients from the foods we eat. If very few dieticians and doctors have any conception of what the ideal might be, where does that leave the average lay person? For those who believe their body needs special help to assure optimum health under present living conditions, we have compiled some information on vitamins and minerals that we have found important for our own use. It may serve as a guideline for people who wish to get started on a program of food supplements. This is still the cheapest health insurance we can buy.

Vitamins

Vitamin A

This vitamin nourishes the body's thin coverings, such as the mucous membranes, respiratory system, and the outer membrane of the eyes. Vitamin A also helps maintain healthy skin, hair, and gums. The body can produce vitamin A from carotene, found in carrots, and from dark green leafy vegetables. One of the best sources is cod liver oil or fish liver oil.

Vitamin B-Complex

Vitamin B is not a single vitamin, but rather a group of related vitamins that work together. Some are called by names, others by number. Most of them are found together in natural foods such as liver, eggs, brewer's yeast, wheat germ, and leafy green vegetables. The B's generally should be taken together when a supplementary form is used.

Vitamin B_1 helps to convert starches and sugar into energy. It is also good for the heart and nerves. A rich source of B_1 is the outer covering of rice and whole grains. When the grains are refined and rice is polished, the B_1 is removed.

Vitamin B_2 is necessary to convert fats, proteins, and carbohydrates into energy. It is valuable for maintaining healthy skin, hair, eyes, and nerves.

Vitamin B_3 is otherwise known as niacin. Niacin is essential for a healthy nervous system. A deficiency of this vitamin can result in headaches, insomnia, and depression. Some success has been reported in administering high doses to hyperactive children. Niacin is also used in the treatment of schizophrenia.

Vitamin B_6 is found in soybeans. This vitamin helps regulate the salt and water balances of the body. It helps regulate cholesterol levels and like the other B's it also plays an active role in maintaining a healthy nervous system.

Vitamin B_{12} is contained in meat, saltwater fish, oysters, and dairy products. It contributes to red blood cell formation and is essential for proper growth in children. A deficiency can result in poor appetite and pernicious anemia.

Biotin is one of the B vitamins produced by the body, provided the digestive system is in optimum condition. However, if antibiotics or drugs are used, they destroy the friendly intestinal bacteria.

Cultured milk products, like yogurt, should be taken to help the intestines return to normal functioning in this respect.

Choline enables the body to put its fat deposits to use. It helps to regulate and control blood pressure. By metabolizing fats, choline stimulates the body's production of lecithin, which in turn helps control cholesterol levels in blood. Large amounts of this vitamin are needed.

Inositol comes from the same sources and performs most of the same functions as choline. Animals lacking inositol in experiments show loss of hair.

Pantothenic Acid is particularly valuable for its antistress activities. It is highly recommended in the prevention of mental disease. It has been useful in the treatment of arthritis and allergies, and is beneficial to the digestive system.

PABA (*Para-Amino-Benzoic Acid*) is one of the B vitamins whose function in the body is not yet well understood. It seems to have a relationship to hair color and helpful in certain skin conditions. It is the best sun-screen agent known when applied in an ointment on the skin.

B_{15} and B_{17} are the two controversial B vitamins. Research on these has been done mostly outside the United States. The Russians have used B_{15} in treating circulatory problems and heart disease with reported success. B_{17} is sometimes called Laetrile. Laetrile has not been accepted as a treatment for cancer in the USA. B_{17} is banned by the government because it is not recognized as having any benefits. B_{15} has been on and off the market in this country. It is found in rice polishings, whole grains, and brewer's yeast. B_{17} is found in seeds of most fruits. The kernel of the apricot is a particularly rich source. Like B_{12} this vitamin is not found in brewer's yeast.

Vitamin C

Vitamin C is probably the best known of all. The list of its benefits is almost endless. Here is a sample of the ways it has been used with success: fighting infections, including colds; for allergies, arthritis, poisonous insect bites, gum diseases, calcium deposits, mononucleosis, and back problems.

The complete vitamin C complex includes Bioflavonoids (sometimes called vitamin P). Whether it is actually a separate vitamin or a part of vitamin C, it works closely together with C. Bioflavonoids provide benefits which plain vitamin C does not. They strengthen the tiny capillaries and act as an anticoagulant. Bioflavonoids have also been reported to be effective in the treatment of rheumatic fever, hemorrhoids, hemorrhages, hardening of the arteries, and varicose veins.

Vitamin D

The major source of vitamin D is sunlight. The only dependable source we have year round is cod liver or fish liver oil. Vitamin D is helpful in the treatment of psoriasis and without it the body does not make proper use of calcium. Vitamin D can be toxic when taken in huge doses, say 50,000 to 100,000 mgs. daily. However, the taste of cod liver oil makes this an unlikely occurrence.

Vitamin E

One of the vitamins almost completely missing from today's foods. Wheat germ, for example, the richest source of E, is removed in the milling of white flour. Vitamin E is also found in seed, soybeans and some nuts. Vitamin E is useful in the treatment of varicose veins and heart problems as an effective anticoagulant. This vitamin also improves circulation. We have found it to work like a miracle in treating burns and in healing wounds when applied locally. It also brings relief from pain and helps heal scar tissue. Vitamin E is available in natural form under the name d-alpha tocopherol.

Minerals

Calcium

The best sources of calcium are milk and other dairy products. Some calcium is also available in green vegetables, nuts, and eggs.

Besides playing a part in strengthening bones and teeth, calcium also helps to keep nerves calm and to regulate heart rhythm. Calcium is dissolved in an acid medium and needs the presence of vitamin D. A good source of calcium, particularly for older people, is bone meal purchased in tablet or powder form.

Magnesium

This is a mineral found in nuts, whole grains, peas, and soybean products. Magnesium is an antacid. It has been effective in treatment of prostate conditions, and used successfully to treat emotional and mental problems. It is useful for neuromuscular quieting.

Phosphorus

Phosphorus is related to calcium and must work together with it. It is good to keep the calcium intake high because as phosphorus is excreted from the body, calcium is taken along. Phosphorus is abundant in meat, eggs, nuts, lecithin, and brewer's yeast. It helps nerve and muscular activity, essential for good brain functioning and the building of strong bones and teeth.

Potassium

An important mineral in regulating body liquids, it is also needed for muscular activity. The richest sources are raw fruits and vegetables. It should always be in balance with sodium as they two work together. An excess of one can cause a depletion of the other.

Zinc

One of the trace minerals necessary for proper growth and sexual development. It seems to promote rapid healing of wounds and aids the body in resisting disease. Zinc is found in oysters, lentils, beans, and perhaps most richly in pumpkin seeds.

Iodine

The source of iodine is sea kelp. Kelp contains iodine along with many other trace minerals. Iodine is necessary for good health of the thyroid gland.

Appendix III: High-Vitality Foods

Yogurt

A cultured milk product which contains enzymes to aid digestion and encourages the utilization of calcium and absorption of protein. It provides a factorylike setting for the production of B vitamins within the body. Yogurt can easily be made at home.

Wheat Germ

The embryo of the grain of wheat and thus its vital center. Wheat germ is one of the best sources of B vitamins, protein and minerals. Vitamin E is extracted from wheat germ. When white flour is milled the germ is removed, robbing it of a large part of its inherent food value. Wheat germ can be bought in health food stores. One small warning, however! Make sure it has been refrigerated so that its natural oils have been kept fresh. Wheat germ can be added to other cereals, breads, pancakes, and cookies, or used in place of bread crumbs.

Brewer's Yeast

One of the most potent and concentrated sources of vitamins and minerals. It contains almost the entire B complex (except for B_{12}) and is a complete protein. It contains no sugar, fats, or starches.

Yeast powder or flakes can be added to batters for bread and biscuits or to casseroles. It is also used in a pep-up drink. Just stir some yeast into tomato juice or broth.

Lecithin

A powerful fat emulsifier which helps to break up cholesterol. Lecithin is an extract from soybeans and can be bought in granular form, powder, liquid, or capsules. It is a good source of protective elements, particularly for the heart and arteries. Lecithin contains vitamin E and two of the B vitamins, choline and inositol. It increases gamma globulin in the blood supply, thereby strengthening the protective forces of the body against diseases.

Honey

A truly natural food and one of the few natural sweeteners. Besides containing countless vitamins, minerals, and enzymes, honey possesses bacteria-destroying properties. These things, however, are true only of pollen honey manufactured by bees in their natural way. Much of the "grade A" honey may be nothing more than sugar water.

Seeds

Contain the secret of life. They are a gold mine for many minerals and vitamins, especially the B vitamins, as well as A and E. They are among the best sources of unsaturated fatty acids. Pumpkin seeds and sunflower seeds are particularly rich in zinc, the trace mineral which is wiped out of every refined and processed food.

Sprouts

Germinated from seeds, their nutritional contents are increased by up to 1000 percent. Sprouts contain an abundance of B vitamins, as well as A and E, lots of minerals and protein. Seeds can be sprouted at home and added to salads, sandwiches, soups, or eaten by the handful as a delicious snack. Instructions on methods of sprouting and many varieties of seeds are available at most health food stores.

Appendix IV: Sources of Biological Medicine

1. Allergies

Body, Mind and Sugar, E. M. Abrahamson and A. W. Pezet (New York: Pyramid Books, 1951), chap. 4.

Nature's Cures, Carlson Wade (New York: Universal Publishing and Distributing Corporation, 1972), chap. 5.

2. Alcoholism

Alcoholism: The Nutritional Approach, Roger J. Williams (Austin: The University of Texas Press, 1959).

Megavitamin Therapy, Ruth Adams and Frank Murray (New York: Larchmont Books, 1973), chap. 4.

New Hope for Incurable Disease, E. Cheraskin and W. M. Ringsdorf (New York: Exposition Press, 1971), chap. 5.

3. Arthritis and Rheumatism

Nutrition Against Disease, Roger J. Williams (New York: Pitman Publishing Corporation, 1971), chap. 8.

There IS a Cure for Arthritis, Paavo O. Airola (West Nyack, N.Y.: Parker Publishing Co., 1968).
Vitamin B_6, The Doctor's Report, John M. Ellis and James Presley (New York: Harper & Row, 1973), chap. 3.

4. Colds and Flu

A New Breed of Doctor, Alan H. Nittler (New York: Pyramid House, 1972), pp. 101–102.
Vitamin C and the Common Cold, Linus Pauling (San Francisco: W. H. Freeman and Company, 1970).

5. Constipation and Colitis

How to Get Well, Paavo Airola (Phoenix, Ariz.: Health Plus, 1974), pp. 64–65.
Nutrition: Your Key to Good Health, Carlton Fredericks (N. Hollywood, Calif.: London Press, 1964), pp. 93–99.

6. Dental Problems

Nutrition Against Disease, Roger Williams, chap. 7.

7. Fatigue

Body, Mind, and the B Vitamins, Ruth Adams and Frank Murray (New York: Larchmont Books, 1972).
Know Your Nutrition, Linda Clark (New Canaan, Conn.: Keats Publishing, 1973), chap. 6.
Treasury of Secrets, Gayelord Hauser (Greenwich, Conn.: Fawcett Publications, 1951), chap. 11.

8. Hypoglycemia

A New Breed of Doctor, Alan H. Nittler, chap. 6.
Body, Mind, and Sugar, E. M. Abrahamson and A. W. Pezet, the whole book.
Megavitamin Therapy, Ruth Adams and Frank Murray, chap. 12.

9. Heart Disease

Nutrition Against Disease, Roger J. Williams, chap. 5.
Vitamin E for Ailing and Healthy Hearts, Wilfrid E. Shute (New York: Pyramid House Publishers, 1969).

10. Hyperactive Children

Body, Mind, and the B Vitamins, Ruth Adams and Frank Murray, chap. 5.
Megavitamin Therapy, Ruth Adams and Frank Murray, chap. 10.
Why Your Child is Hyperactive, Ben F. Feingold (New York: Random House, 1974).

11. Insomnia

Treasury of Secrets, Gayelord Hauser, pp. 209–211.

12. Stress and Hypertension

How to Get Well, Paavo Airola, pp. 109–111.

13. Prostate Gland

The Complete Question-and-Answer Book of Natural Therapy, Gary Null and Staff (New York: Dell Publishing Co., 1972), pp. 89–95.
The Prostate, J. I. Rodale (Emmaus, Penn.: Rodale Press, Inc., 1972).

14. Schizophrenia and Depression

Megavitamin Therapy, Ruth Adams and Frank Murray, chap. 9.
Nutrition Against Disease, Roger J. Williams, chap. 10.

15. Overweight

Nutrition Against Disease, Roger J. Williams, chap. 6.
Treasury of Secrets, Gayelord Hauser, chap. 24.

www.ingramcontent.com/pod-product-compliance
Lightning Source LLC
LaVergne TN
LVHW010932100826
845153LV00001B/5

* 9 7 8 1 5 3 2 6 1 2 6 8 8 *